ANOTHER 250 BEST

muffin

RECIPES

ANOTHER 250 BEST muffin RECIPES

Esther Brody

Another 250 best muffin recipes

For complete cataloguing information, see page 6.

DESIGN, EDITORIAL AND PRODUCTION:	MATTHEWS COMMUNICATIONS DESIGN INC.
PHOTOGRAPHY:	MARK T. SHAPIRO
ART DIRECTION, FOOD PHOTOGRAPHY:	SHARON MATTHEWS
FOOD STYLIST:	KATE BUSH
PROP STYLIST:	CHARLENE ERRICSON
MANAGING EDITOR:	PETER MATTHEWS
INDEX:	BARBARA SCHON
COLOR SCANS & FILM:	POINTONE GRAPHICS

Cover photo: BERRY OAT BRAN MUFFINS (PAGE 122)

We acknowledge the financial support of the Government of Canada through the Book Publishing Industry Development Program (BPIDP) for our publishing activities.
Canada

Published by: Robert Rose Inc. • 120 Eglinton Avenue East, Suite 1000, Toronto, Ontario, Canada M4P 1E2 Tel: (416) 322-6552

Printed in Canada
34567 FP 07 06 05 04

Contents

Canadian Cataloguing in Publication Data

Brody, Esther
  Another 250 best muffin recipes

Includes index.
ISBN 0-7788-0020-2

1. Muffins. I. Title.

TX770.M83B76 2000   641.8'15   C00-931301-X

Dedication

To my son Leonard Jason,
who spent many, many hours of his time,
in the midst of a very busy law practice, to make
all of this possible for me.

To my daughter, Lisa Michelle,
for bringing such joy and happiness into my
life with the birth of my first grandchild, beautiful
little Natalie Arielle, the love of my life.

To Bob Dees of Robert Rose Inc.,
for his kindness, his guidance and expertise,
his faith in my book and his hard work to make
it such a success.

In memory of my parents,
Mary and Louis Goldstein,
who gave so much to their children.

Introduction

The Muffin Lady is back! And I've got with another 250 delicious recipes that I'm sure you're going to love.

I was thrilled by the warm reception my first book, *The 250 Best Muffin Recipes,* received. It seems that muffins really are popular. And no wonder — they are endlessly adaptable. Muffins are great to eat at any time of the day, whether for breakfast, as an addition to lunch or a welcome snack. Muffins can be healthy and nutritious — using bran, whole wheat, oats and fruit — or not-so-healthy (but oh-so-yummy) — using chocolate, icing and syrup. Muffins can be prepared quickly using ingredients you usually have on hand and need to use up, such as overripe bananas or other perishable fruits such as strawberries, peaches or nectarines. The possibilities are endless. So use your imagination. Choose a recipe and feel free to add your own unique twist to it.

Happy baking!

Esther Brody

Easy Steps to Perfect Muffins

To achieve perfect baking results, just follow these basic steps:

- Read the recipe carefully and check the required ingredients, oven temperature and baking time.

- Remove shortening, butter or margarine from the refrigerator 1 hour before mixing. Unless the recipe states otherwise, take milk and eggs out of the refrigerator as you start mixing.

- Adjust the oven racks to the desired level. I always bake muffins or cakes in the middle of the oven on the center rack.

- Preheat oven thoroughly to the recommended temperature in your recipe. This is important for maximum rise; a too-cool temperature will result in nearly flat muffins.

- Collect all of the utensils that you will require.

- Set out the remaining ingredients that you will need.

- Prepare the muffin tins. You can grease them, spray them with vegetable spray or, as I prefer, line the tins with paper baking cups.

- Check the recipe again for the method of baking to be used.

- Spoon the batter into greased or paper-lined muffin tins, filling two-thirds to three-quarters full. Any cups not filled with batter should be filled halfway with water. This will not only save the muffin pans but will add moisture to the oven, enlarging the muffins and allowing for even baking.

- Bake as your recipe directs. Muffins are done when they are golden brown, firm to the touch, come away from the sides of the pan and a toothpick inserted in the center comes out clean and dry.

The Essentials of Muffin Making

Successful muffin making depends on three important activities — measuring, mixing and baking. Let's look at each of these in turn.

MEASURING

For best baking results, it is essential to measure ingredients accurately each time.

Have measuring cups for both dry and liquid ingredients ready — it saves time to have large measures also.

Make sure that your measuring spoons are in good shape, not warped, bent or dented, as you can't get perfect measurements if they are.

DRY INGREDIENTS

Use measuring cups with a flat rim so the ingredients can be easily leveled off.

Use aluminum or plastic sets that hold the exact amount needed when leveled off.

For less than 1/4 cup (50 mL) use your standard measuring spoons.

Fill standard measuring cups or spoons to overflowing, then level off using a straight-edged knife or spatula — do not pack or bang on table.

FLOUR. We know that flour, no matter what type, is never sifted before it is measured. Any dry ingredients (like salt, baking powder or baking soda) should be sifted with the flour.

When a recipe calls for "sifted" flour, it should be sifted first and then measured.

If a recipe calls for "sifting the dry ingredients together," there is no need to sift the flour prior to measuring. Just sift all pre-measured dry ingredients together and proceed with the recipe.

You can use a scoop or spoon to add flour to the measuring cup. When it is full, level off any excess with the straight edge of a knife.

I find that the best way to measure flour is to choose a measure of the correct size with a flush rim for leveling. Fill it to overflowing by dipping it into the package directly. Do not bang the measuring cup on the table, but level off with the straight edge of a knife or spatula.

Older cookbooks call for flour to be sifted before measuring but today most flours are pre-sifted.

BAKING POWDER AND BAKING SODA. Dip measuring spoon into container and level off with the edge of a knife.

To measure 1/8 tsp (0.5 mL), halve 1/4 tsp (1 mL) with the tip of a knife.

Dry ingredients such as baking soda, baking powder and cocoa sometimes have a tendency to pack down in their containers so before measuring, stir to loosen.

BROWN SUGAR. If a recipe calls for "firmly packed" brown sugar, spoon into a measuring cup, pack it down firmly with the back of a spoon and then level off.

LIQUID INGREDIENTS

Always use a see-through glass or plastic measure with volume amounts marked on the outside.

Place glass measuring cup on a flat surface. Bend down so that you can read the measure at eye level.

Make sure that your liquid measuring cup has a safety rim above the full cup mark in order to get an accurate measurement without spilling a drop.

OIL OR MELTED FAT. Dip measuring spoon into the oil and then lift out carefully. The spoon should be so full that it will not hold another drop.

SHORTENING. Partly fill a measuring cup with water, leaving space for the amount of shortening to be measured. Add shortening until the water moves up to the 1 cup (250 mL) mark or press the shortening firmly into the fractional cup so that no air holes are left. Level off and scoop out.

MIXING

A key factor in producing successful muffins is the mixing. Your muffins will be lighter when you mix them together quickly and lightly as this produces the best rising effect.

When a muffin batter is overmixed it is too smooth and flows readily leaving the spoon in a long ribbon-like strand. This will result in tough muffins with funnels and a pronounced peak. Muffins should always be light and tender and baked to a golden brown. The secret for accomplishing this is not to overmix or stir. Use as few strokes as possible — the batter should look lumpy. I stir and mix my muffin batter with a "folding-in" movement using a large stainless steel spoon, not a spatula as you would normally when "folding" in a recipe.

In most of my muffin recipes I fill the muffin tins full, right to the top, unless I am adding a filling or topping, to produce large and even-sized muffins.

I prefer to use the standard method with most of my recipes, unless the recipe states otherwise. I find it the easiest way.

Dry ingredients should be thoroughly mixed in one bowl and liquid ingredients in another bowl. When separated like this they can be left indefinitely. But as soon as you combine the two of them, you have to work quickly, stirring just to enough to moisten and combine. Then spoon immediately into muffin tins.

The batter for muffins is usually stirred but may be creamed.

For a stirred batter, the dry ingredients are mixed together in order to evenly distribute the baking powder and baking soda. If the leavening is unevenly distributed, the muffins may have a bitter taste.

For a creamed batter, the shortening and sugar are beaten together before adding the other ingredients. The muffins are usually sweeter and have a cake-like texture.

Once the muffin batter has been prepared and put into the muffin tins it should go into the oven quickly. The idea is for the batter to start rising in the oven not on the counter. That is why I prepare the muffin tins before I start mixing the recipe and I have all of the ingredients ready, including any grating.

BAKING

There are two common methods for baking muffins in a conventional oven (for microwave baking tips, see pages 16 to 19):

THE STANDARD METHOD

1. Sift the dry ingredients into a large bowl and make a well or depression in the center. Remember to mix dry ingredients together well in order to distribute the baking powder and baking soda evenly.

2. Combine the egg (slightly beaten), milk and oil or melted shortening (cool the melted butter or shortening first).

3. Add the liquid ingredients all at once to the dry ingredients.

4. Stir quickly only until the dry ingredients are moist. The batter will be slightly lumpy.

5. Spoon batter into prepared muffin tins, filling two-thirds full.

6. Bake as directed.

THE BISCUIT METHOD

1. Cut shortening into the sifted dry ingredients until crumbly.

2. Combine the egg and milk. Add all at once to the flour mixture.

3. Stir just until moist.

4. Spoon batter into prepared muffin tins, filling two-thirds full.

5. Bake as directed. Most muffin recipes suggest baking at 375° F (190° C) or 400° F (200° C). I have found that baking at 425° F (220° C) for 20 minutes works best for my muffins.

If the muffins brown too quickly turn your oven down.

Muffins bake best on the middle rack in the oven. On the lowest shelf the bottoms burn too quickly and on the highest shelf the tops brown too soon.

I set my timer for 15 minutes and then I turn the muffin pan around in the oven, putting front to back. Then I set the timer for 5 minutes and bake for the remaining 5 minutes.

Most ovens cook unevenly, but I have found that my method of turning for the last 5 minutes of baking produces a more evenly baked and browned muffin.

Check the accuracy of your oven often and make any necessary adjustments. It is quite normal for ovens to vary. Also, ovens often bake faster at the back, that is why I turn the muffin pan around for a more even baking.

Muffins straight from the hot oven are very fragile so allow the pan to cool for about 5 to 10 minutes before removing the muffins from the pan. The steam from the pan should loosen them. If they still stick, loosen the muffins by running a knife around the edge of the cup. Often you can simply turn the pan upside-down and the muffins will fall out.

If you are baking fruit-filled muffins, cool completely before removing them from the tins.

If you wish to keep muffins hot for serving, loosen them and tilt to one side of the muffin tin slightly. It is a good idea to place them in the warm, turned off oven until you are ready to serve.

When Muffins Go Wrong...

Can't figure out why your muffins don't look and taste as they should? Consider the following.

Problem: Muffins are too hard.

There is too much flour and not enough liquid. Try using 1/4 cup (50 mL) less flour.

You may have stirred too long and hard. Try mixing for only 10 seconds.

Problem: Muffins are flat or spreading.

If they are spreading out all over the top of the tins, don't fill as full.

There could be too much liquid in the batter. Try using 1/4 cup (50 mL) less liquid.

Problem: Muffins are tough and soggy, peaks in center.

You have probably overmixed, which toughens the batter. Underbaking could also be the cause of the problem. Ovens vary in temperature, so try increasing the temperature by 25 degrees and shortening the baking time.

Problem: Muffins rise high, fall flat in center.

There is not enough flour. Increase the amount by about 1/4 cup (50 mL). Sometimes the eggs are so large that they increase the ratio of liquid ingredients. Use large eggs but not extra large.

Problem: Muffins do not brown.

Your oven rack is too high or too low.

If muffins are baked on the lowest rack, they may burn on the bottom before being done on top.

If muffins are baked on the highest rack, they will get too brown on top.

Always use the middle rack for an even browning.

Problem: Muffins are coarse-textured.

This is usually caused by insufficient stirring and baking at too low a temperature.

Microwave Muffins

Muffins baked in a microwave oven can be just as delicious as those made the traditional way. The main difference is the speed at which they can be prepared. Microwaves are also great for defrosting and reheating frozen food and for refreshing stale cakes and muffins, as well as breads.

Most conventional-oven recipes can easily be adapted for use in a microwave. Try to choose recipes that you know well, at first, until you become more familiar with adapting recipes. It is much easier to work out changes required if you know what the final result should be. If you did not enjoy a particular muffin prepared in the conventional way, you will probably not like it any better when baked in the microwave.

- Most foods cook faster in a microwave than in a conventional oven. This is particularly true of baked products, like muffins, which cook in a very short time (in fact, you can have piping hot muffins ready to eat in 5 minutes). As a result, however, they do not surface brown. You can improve their appearance by frosting, or using a topping such as cinnamon or nuts.

- Liquid ingredients slow down microwave cooking, whereas sugars and fatty ingredients will cook more rapidly. Therefore, to adapt a conventional recipe to the microwave, you must adjust the amount of liquid and fat to obtain the right balance between the two.

- Timing is very important. Just 2 or 3 minutes of extra cooking will dehydrate and toughen many foods in the microwave.

- A "carry-over" cooking time is required for almost every item cooked in the microwave. This is a few minutes during which the food rests, after being removed from the microwave, to allow it to finish cooking. Allow muffins, 1 or 2 minutes. Follow your recipe. It is surprising how much cooking occurs during this carry-over time.

- Frozen muffins (and other foods) can be easily defrosted in the microwave when needed; reheating helps food retain the flavor often lost with conventional reheating.

- The inside of the microwave oven stays cool, so spills won't bake on and can be wiped clean with a damp cloth or paper towel. If any food should stick on the oven walls, place 1 cup (250 mL) of water in the oven and heat for 2 1/2 to 3 minutes. This produces steam which will soften the spills so that they can then be wiped clean.

- Cleaning baking dishes after microwave cooking is easier and quicker because food does not stick to them as it does in conventional cooking.

- Keep your microwave oven clean; any food left on the walls or bottom will absorb microwave energy and therefore increase cooking times.

- Microwave cooking is more efficient; it requires only about half the electrical energy used in conventional cooking. With microwave cooking, the food gets hot but the kitchen, oven, baking dishes, utensils — and you, the cook — stay cool. And because the dish or container doesn't get hot, foods cooked in a microwave also cool down fast.

🧁 **Never** use any container made of metal in the microwave, or one that has a metal trim. Glass, glass ceramic, heat-resistant glass or plastic containers can be used.

🧁 The muffin maker, or cupcaker pan, is designed especially for microwave oven use. If it has a cup in the center, **do not** use it, since microwave energy is least efficient in the center of the oven and the muffin will not be properly cooked.

🧁 To determine if a dish or container is suitable for use in the microwave oven, place 1 cup (250 mL) of tap water in the empty dish or container to be tested. Place it in the oven. Heat for 30 to 60 seconds. If the water becomes hot and the dish does not, then it is suitable for microwave use. If the dish becomes hot, it can't be used for microwave cooking.

🧁 **Hint:** If you do not have a cupcaker (microwave muffin pan) or glass ramekins, use the lower part of a paper cup for hot drinks. Cut it down to size and line it with a paper baking cup. Place the cups in a circle on a flat microwave-safe plate, and use as you would ramekins.

🧁 Shallow containers produce better results than deep ones. Round shapes are better than square or rectangular containers. (Food has a tendency to overcook in the corners because more microwave energy is absorbed there.)

🧁 The cooking pattern in foods cooked in microwave ovens tends to be circular, with a hole in the middle, similar to a doughnut. The center of the dish receives the least amount of microwave energy and thus is slower to cook. It is often recommended that a glass be placed right-side up in the center of the dish so that there will be no uncooked spot in the center.

🧁 Use large baking cups and fill them two-thirds full. If you put more batter in, they may overflow during baking and the muffins could be undercooked. The cooking time given in most microwave muffin recipes is correct for the amount of batter that fits comfortably into this size of baking cup. Cups of a different size will not yield as good results.

🧁 To ensure even cooking, give the muffin pan a half turn during the cooking period. Another technique for even cooking is to place your muffin or dish **on a rack**. For example, if you put 6 ramekins with muffin batter in the microwave oven, they should be arranged in a ring and their position changed during cooking time. The individual cups are not rotated. The circle of ramekins is turned for better distribution of heat energy.

🧁 When muffins are done, tiny bubbles will pop on the surface (as on the tops of pancakes when they are ready to turn). The muffins may be slightly moist on top, but when scratched with a toothpick, the dough will be done beneath the surface and the small moist spots will disappear when the muffins stand for a few minutes.

🧁 **Hint:** For mini-micro muffins, line a paper (but not recycled paper) or styrofoam egg carton with mini paper baking cups. Fill only two-thirds full also. Microwave on High for 1 to 1 1/2 minutes or until tops are dry.

With technology changing so rapidly, each year newer and better microwave ovens are appearing on the market, so always read the instruction booklet very carefully. If your microwave oven comes with a revolving turntable, it is still wise to shift or rotate your muffin pan halfway during cooking, unless you know for certain that there are no hot spots and that the heat is distributed evenly. In most ovens, there are hot spots, so shifting or rotating will ensure even cooking.

A simple test to see where the hot spots are in your oven is to lay slices of bread out to cover the bottom or turntable. Place pieces of cheese to cover the bread slices. Cook on High for about 2 minutes. You will be able to identify the hot spots in your oven by where the cheese is melting.

Being a creature of habit, I do most of my muffin baking in a regular oven and therefore don't have an abundance of recipes for the microwave oven, but I hope you will enjoy the ones I have included in this chapter, and that you will try adapting some of your recipes.

Here's a quick summary of what to remember when baking muffins in your microwave:

- Prepare muffin batter according to your recipe directions.

- Use a microwave cupcaker special pan, or paper-cup lined ramekins, for a proper shape. Use the large size.

- Place your ramekins or cupcaker pan, on a rack in the oven and rotate or turn it halfway through the cooking time to ensure even cooking.

- Check your recipe for correct cooking time.

- Test for doneness with a toothpick inserted near the center of a muffin. It should come out clean.

- Let muffin pan or ramekins stand on a flat surface, covered, to finish baking, for about 5 to 10 minutes. (The required time is 1 to 2 minutes, but I find better results leaving them for 5 to 10 minutes).

- Remember that the technique and bakeware required, as well as the end results, will differ when using a microwave rather than a standard oven.

Get to know your microwave. Ovens range in wattage from 500 to 720 watts (or more). The higher wattage ovens heat foods faster; if you have a lower wattage, cooking times will be longer. If you don't know the wattage of your oven, check the back of the oven to see if there is a silver plate with the number on it; Failing that, a quick way to estimate the wattage is to see how long it takes to bring 1 cup (250 mL) of tap water to a boil in a glass measure. It should take 2 1/2 to 3 minutes in a 600- to 720-watt oven, 4 minutes in a 500- to 600-watt oven, and 5 minutes in a 400- to 500-watt oven.

Microwaves, like radio waves, pass through food but are stopped when they encounter moisture. The wave cause the water molecules to vibrate at a tremendous rate, which causes friction and thus heat. This cooks the food. Most microwave recipes give you a range of cooking times. Choose the lesser amount, then check for doneness, otherwise overcooking may be a problem.

Hint: For a quick café-au-lait with your muffins, microwave 1 cup (250 mL) milk on High for 2 to 3 minutes. Pour in 1/4 cup (50 mL) espresso coffee or 1 tsp (5 mL) instant coffee.

Micro-Tips

TO SHELL NUTS:

Pour 1 cup (250 mL) nuts (brazil, walnuts, almonds or pecans) into a large bowl. Cover with 1 cup (250 mL) water and heat on High 3 to 4 minutes, or until water boils. Let stand for 1 minute. Pour off water and arrange nuts on paper towel to cool. Use a nutcracker to shell the nuts, being careful that you aren't burned by any hot water that may still be inside the shell.

TO SOFTEN BROWN SUGAR:

Put the brown sugar in a covered container and microwave on High for 50 seconds.

or

Put the hard block of sugar into a heavy plastic bag. Add a little water, or a quarter of an apple, or a slice of bread. Tie a piece of string loosely around the opening and heat on High for 20 seconds. Check to see if sugar has softened. If not, repeat once or twice, as necessary, being sure not to let sugar melt. When the sugar has softened sufficiently, take it out of the oven and allow to stand for about 5 minutes. Remove apple or bread and throw away, then stir to remove lumps.

or

Remove hard brown sugar from package and place on a plate with an apple wedge. Cover and cook on High for 20 to 30 seconds. Let stand 30 seconds, then uncover and stir to remove lumps.

TO EXTRACT JUICE FROM A LEMON:

Microwave the whole lemon on High for 30 seconds, then roll firmly on a flat surface, using the palm of your hand.

TO THAW FROZEN JUICE CONCENTRATE:

Place frozen concentrated juice in a small bowl (never microwave in metal can) and microwave on High for 1 minute.

TO MELT CHOCOLATE:

Place chocolate in a glass measuring cup. Microwave on Medium-High for 1 minute, then stir and repeat until melted completely. It will take about 2 minutes to melt 1 cup (250 mL) of chocolate chips.

TO MELT BUTTER OR MARGARINE:

Place in a glass dish. Cover with wax paper or a paper towel to avoid splattering. Heat on High for 30-second intervals until fully melted.

FOR ROOM TEMPERATURE BUTTER:

Cover 1/4 cup (50 mL) butter with waxed paper. Microwave on Defrost for 30 seconds.

TO LIQUEFY SOLID HONEY:

Place in a glass cup or container, Cook on High for 30 seconds, then stir to dissolve the crystals; repeat procedure, stirring often, until the honey is liquid.

FOR SPREADABLE CRYSTALLIZED HONEY:

Remove lid from jar and microwave on High for 1 to 2 minutes.

TO SOFTEN CREAM CHEESE:

For spreads and dips, or baking – microwave, uncovered, on Defrost for 1 to 2 minutes.

TO BRING CHEESE TO ROOM TEMPERATURE:

Place 8 oz (250 g) cold cheese on a microwave-safe plate. Microwave on Medium for 45 to 60 seconds until surface no longer feels chilled.

TO PLUMP RAISINS (OR DRIED FRUITS):

Microwave 1 cup (250 mL) raisins or dried fruits in 1/2 cup (125 mL) water, covered, on High for 2 minutes or until boiling. Let stand, covered, for 10 minutes.

or

Place raisins or dried fruits in a small bowl and sprinkle with water or other liquid. Cook, uncovered, on High for 15 to 30 seconds, depending on amount.

Apple Spice Muffins

1/4 cup	shortening	50 mL
3/4 cup	granulated sugar	175 mL
2	eggs	2
3/4 cup	applesauce	175 mL
1/4 cup	milk	50 mL
1 tbsp	lemon juice	15 mL
1 1/2 cups	flour	375 mL
1 tsp	salt	5 mL
1 tsp	baking soda	5 mL
1 tsp	cinnamon	5 mL
1/4 tsp	ground nutmeg	1 mL
1/4 tsp	ground cloves	1 mL
1/4 cup	floured raisins	50 mL
1/4 cup	chopped walnuts	50 mL

Microwave muffin pan, paper-lined

1. In a bowl cream together shortening and sugar. Add eggs and mix well. Add applesauce, milk and lemon juice.

2. In another bowl, sift together flour, salt and baking soda. Add cinnamon, nutmeg and cloves. Pour this dry mixture gradually into the liquid mixture. Add raisins and nuts and mix together.

3. Spoon batter into prepared muffin pan. Bake on High for 2 to 2 1/2 minutes, turning halfway through cooking time. Let stand for 3 to 5 minutes.

Banana Oatmeal Muffins

1/4 cup	butter or margarine, softened	50 mL
3/4 cup	packed brown sugar	175 mL
1	egg, beaten	1
1 cup	buttermilk	250 mL
1 cup	rolled oats	250 mL
1 cup	all-purpose flour	250 mL
1 tbsp	baking powder	15 mL
1/2 tsp	salt	2 mL
1/2 tsp	ground allspice	2 mL
2	medium bananas, chopped	2

Ramekins or microwave muffin pan, paper-lined

1. In a bowl cream together butter and brown sugar. Mix in egg and buttermilk.

2. In another bowl, combine oats, flour, baking powder, salt and allspice; mix well. Add to the creamed mixture and stir in the bananas.

3. Spoon batter into prepared ramekins or muffin pan, filling cups one-half to two-thirds full. (If using ramekins, arrange in microwave in a circle). Microwave on High for about 2 minutes, rotating after 1 minute. A toothpick inserted in the center should come out clean and dry. Let muffins stand for 3 to 5 minutes before removing from pan.

Banana Pecan Oat Muffins

1 cup	all-purpose flour	250 mL
1/4 cup	oat bran	50 mL
1/4 cup	packed brown sugar	50 mL
1/4 cup	chopped pecans	50 mL
1/2 tsp	baking soda	2 mL
Pinch	salt	Pinch
1 cup	mashed bananas (about 3 medium)	250 mL
1	egg	1
1/2 cup	oil	125 mL
TOPPING		
3 tbsp	chopped pecans	45 mL
3 tbsp	packed brown sugar	45 mL
1/4 tsp	cinnamon	1 mL

Microwave muffin pan, paper-lined

1. In a large bowl combine flour, oat bran, sugar, pecans, baking soda and salt.

2. In a smaller bowl, beat together bananas, egg and oil. Stir this mixture into the flour mixture just until blended. Spoon batter into prepared muffin pan, filling cups two-thirds full.

3. In a bowl combine pecans, sugar and cinnamon and sprinkle evenly over muffins.

4. Bake on High, rotating twice, for 2 minutes or until toothpick inserted in center comes out clean and dry. Let stand for 3 to 5 minutes.

Blueberry Quick Oat Muffins

1/2 cup	granulated sugar	125 mL
1 1/4 cups	all-purpose flour	300 mL
1 cup	uncooked quick oats	250 mL
1 1/2 tsp	baking powder	7 mL
1/2 tsp	baking soda	2 mL
3/4 cup	sour cream	175 mL
1/3 cup	margarine, melted	75 mL
1/3 cup	milk	75 mL
1	egg, beaten	1
1/2 tsp	vanilla	2 mL
1 cup	fresh blueberries (or frozen, thawed)	250 mL
	SUGAR-CINNAMON MIX (see recipe, page 179)	

Ramekins or microwave muffin pan, paper-lined

1. In a large bowl, combine sugar, flour, oats, baking powder and baking soda.

2. In a smaller bowl, combine sour cream, margarine, milk, egg and vanilla; mix well. Stir this mixture into the dry ingredients, mixing just until moist. Fold in the blueberries.

3. Spoon batter into prepared ramekins or muffin pan, filling cups two-thirds full. Sprinkle with SUGAR-CINNAMON MIX. Bake uncovered on High for 2 1/2 to 3 minutes. A toothpick inserted in the center should come out clean and dry. Let muffins stand for 3 to 5 minutes.

Chocolate Chip Bran Muffins

3/4 cup	milk	175 mL
1/4 cup	oil	50 mL
1	egg, beaten	1
1 cup	bran	250 mL
1 cup	all-purpose flour	250 mL
2 1/2 tsp	baking powder	12 mL
1/2 tsp	salt	2 mL
3 tbsp	cocoa	45 mL
1/2 cup	granulated sugar	125 mL
1/2 cup	chocolate chips	125 mL

Microwave muffin pan, paper-lined

1. In a bowl combine milk, oil and egg. Stir in bran.

2. In another bowl, mix together flour, baking powder, salt and cocoa.

3. Add sugar to the liquid mixture. Stir in flour mixture and add chocolate chips.

4. Spoon batter into prepared muffin pan, filling cups two-thirds full. Place pan on a rack in the microwave. Bake on High for 2 to 2 1/2 minutes, rotating pan halfway through cooking time. Let stand for 3 to 5 minutes before removing from pan.

All Spicy Muffins

1 1/2 cups	all-purpose flour	375 mL
1/2 cup	granulated sugar	125 mL
2 tsp	baking powder	10 mL
1/2 tsp	salt	2 mL
1/2 tsp	ground nutmeg	2 mL
1/2 tsp	ground coriander	2 mL
1/2 tsp	ground allspice	2 mL
1/2 cup	milk	125 mL
1/3 cup	butter or margarine, melted	75 mL
1	egg	1
1/4 cup	granulated sugar	50 mL
1 tsp	ground cinnamon	5 mL
1/4 cup	butter or margarine, melted	50 mL

Microwave muffin pan, double paper-lined

1. In a large bowl, combine flour, 1/2 cup (125 mL) sugar, baking powder, salt, nutmeg, coriander and allspice.

2. In a small bowl, combine milk, 1/3 cup (75 mL) butter and egg. Stir into flour mixture just until moist.

3. Spoon batter into prepared muffin pan, filling three-quarters full. (Baking may have to be done in batches.) Microwave on High for 2 1/2 to 4 1/2 minutes, rotating halfway through cooking time. A toothpick inserted in center should come out clean and dry. Let muffins stand for 5 minutes before removing from pan.

4. Meanwhile, in a small dish combine 1/4 cup (50 mL) sugar and cinnamon. Roll warm muffins in the 1/4 cup (50 mL) melted butter and then the sugar/cinnamon mixture. These muffins are best served warm.

Currant Nut Whole-Wheat Muffins

3/4 cup	all-purpose flour	175 mL
3/4 cup	whole-wheat flour	175 mL
1/3 cup	unprocessed wheat bran, (Miller's bran) *or* oat bran	75 mL
1 tsp	baking soda	5 mL
1/2 tsp	cinnamon	2 mL
1/4 tsp	ground ginger	1 mL
1/4 tsp	salt	1 mL
1 cup	low-fat vanilla yogurt	250 mL
1/4 cup	vegetable oil	50 mL
1	large egg	1
1/4 cup	packed dark brown sugar	50 mL
1/3 cup	chopped walnuts	75 mL
1/3 cup	currants	75 mL

Microwave muffin pan, double paper-lined

1. In a large bowl, mix together all-purpose flour, whole-wheat flour, bran, baking soda, cinnamon, ginger and salt.

2. In a blender or food processor, combine yogurt, oil, egg and sugar; process until smooth. Add half the flour mixture and process until blended. Scrape down sides of container and add remaining flour mixture; process until smooth.

3. Pour batter back into bowl and stir in walnuts and currants. Spoon batter into prepared pan, filling cups three-quarters full. (Baking may have to be done in batches.) Microwave on High for 3 to 4 minutes, rotating muffin pan a quarter-turn twice. Tops should spring back when gently pressed. Let stand for 3 to 5 minutes. There will be moist spots on top but these will dry upon standing.

HINT: The secret to making good microwave muffins is to use crumbs instead of flour — bread, graham cracker or others — or try combining two or more. Flour apparently can cause problems in this type of oven. For example, if your recipe calls for 1 1/2 cups (375 mL) flour, use 1 cup (250 mL) of one type of crumbs and 1/2 cup (125 mL) of another.

"Kentucky" Biscuit Muffins

2 cups	all-purpose flour	500 mL
2 1/2 tsp	baking powder	12 mL
1/2 tsp	baking soda	2 mL
Pinch	salt	Pinch
1 tbsp	granulated sugar	15 mL
1/2 cup	butter *or* margarine *or* shortening	125 mL
3/4 cup	buttermilk	175 mL
1 tbsp	butter, melted	15 mL
	Poppyseeds or fennel seeds, for garnish	

Microwave muffin pan

1. In a large bowl, mix together flour, baking powder, baking soda, salt and sugar. Using a pastry blender, cut in butter until mixture resembles coarse crumbs. Add buttermilk and mix quickly to make a soft dough.

2. Turn dough out onto a lightly floured board and knead a few times to make a soft dough. Do not overknead or the muffins will be hard and dry.

3. Roll the dough out to a square and cut out round biscuits with a glass or cookie cutter; place each in pan. Brush with melted butter and sprinkle with seeds.

4. Bake on High for about 1 1/2 minutes. Let sit for a few minutes and then bake on High for another 1 1/2 minutes. Serve warm. These muffins are great with honey, jam or just butter.

Orange Cinnamon Muffins

2 cups	all-purpose flour	500 mL
1/2 cup	packed brown sugar	125 mL
3 tsp	baking powder	15 mL
1/2 tsp	salt	2 mL
1/2 tsp	cinnamon	2 mL
1 tsp	finely grated orange zest	5 mL
2	eggs	2
1/2 cup	orange juice	125 mL
1/2 cup	vegetable oil	125 mL
TOPPING		
3 tbsp	granulated sugar	45 mL
1 tsp	finely grated orange zest	5 mL
1/2 tsp	cinnamon	2 mL

Microwave muffin pan, paper-lined

1. In a large bowl, combine flour, brown sugar, baking powder, salt, cinnamon and orange zest. Mix well.

2. In a smaller bowl, whisk together eggs, orange juice and oil. Pour into flour mixture and stir just until moist.

3. Spoon batter into prepared muffin pan, filling cups two-thirds full. In a bowl combine sugar, zest and cinnamon; sprinkle over muffins. Bake uncovered on High for 2 to 2 1/2 minutes, rotating pan halfway through cooking time. A toothpick inserted in the center should come out clean and dry. Let muffins stand for 3 to 5 minutes before removing from pan.

Peanut Butter Banana Muffins

1 1/2 cups	all-purpose flour	375 mL
1/2 cup	granulated sugar	125 mL
2 tbsp	baking powder	25 mL
1/2 tsp	salt	2 mL
1	egg, slightly beaten	1
1/2 cup	milk	125 mL
1/3 cup	vegetable oil	75 mL
3/4 cup	mashed banana	175 mL
1 cup	peanut butter chips	250 mL
1/4 cup	raisins	50 mL
1/4 cup	graham cracker crumbs	50 mL

Ramekins, double paper-lined

1. In a large bowl, combine flour, sugar, baking powder and salt. Make a well in the center and add egg, milk, oil and mashed banana; stir just until moist. Stir in peanut butter chips and raisins.

2. Spoon batter into prepared ramekins, filling each half full. Sprinkle with crumbs. (Baking may have to be done in batches.) Arrange ramekins in a circle on rack in microwave and bake on High for 2 minutes. Rotate circle of ramekins and bake for 1 minute or until done.

Pineapple Carrot Nutty Muffins

1 1/2 cups	whole-wheat flour	375 mL
1/2 cup	packed brown sugar	125 mL
1/2 cup	granulated sugar	125 mL
1 cup	Grape Nuts cereal	250 mL
1 1/2 tsp	baking soda	7 mL
3/4 tsp	baking powder	4 mL
2 tsp	cinnamon	10 mL
1 cup	well-drained crushed pineapple	250 mL
2	eggs, beaten	2
2 cups	shredded carrots	500 mL
1 tsp	vanilla	5 mL
3/4 cup	margarine, melted	175 mL

Microwave muffin pan, double paper-lined

1. In a large bowl, combine flour, brown sugar, granulated sugar, cereal, baking soda, baking powder and cinnamon.

2. In a smaller bowl, combine pineapple, eggs, carrots, vanilla and margarine. Stir into the dry ingredients, mixing just until moistened. The batter will be quite thick.

3. Spoon batter into prepared muffin pan, filling cups two-thirds full. Bake, uncovered, on High for 2 to 2 1/2 minutes, rotating halfway through cooking time. Let muffins stand for 3 to 5 minutes before removing from pan.

Quick Poppy Cheese Muffins

2 1/2 cups	all-purpose biscuit mix	625 mL
1 cup	shredded sharp Cheddar cheese	250 mL
1 tsp	poppy seeds	5 mL
1	egg	1
1 cup	milk	250 mL

Ramekins or microwave muffin pan, paper-lined

1. In a large bowl, combine biscuit mix, cheese, poppyseeds, egg and milk; stir just to moisten.

2. Spoon batter into prepared ramekins or pan, filling cups two-thirds full. If using ramekins, arrange them in a circle. Bake on High for 2 1/2 minutes, rotating ramekins or pan halfway through cooking time. Let muffins stand for 3 to 5 minutes.

HINT: An extra apple or two you don't need for baking? A baked apple takes 4 minutes in the microwave. Fill the middle with ice cream and drizzle liqueur on top. A delicious dessert that looks like you spent all day in the kitchen.

Refrigerator Micro-Bran Muffins

This mixture will keep for up to 6 weeks in the refrigerator, ready to use whenever you need fresh muffins.

1 1/2 cups	Bran flakes	375 mL
1 1/2 cups	cooking bran	375 mL
1/2 cup	boiling water	125 mL
2	eggs, slightly beaten	2
1/4 cup	molasses	50 mL
1 3/4 cups	buttermilk *or* sour milk	425 mL
1/4 cup	oil	50 mL
1 to 2 tsp	browning sauce (such as Crosse and Blackwell)	5 to 10 mL
1 cup	raisins *or* dates *or* currants *or* prunes	250 mL
2 1/2 tsp	baking soda	12 mL
1 tsp	baking powder	5 mL
1/4 tsp	salt	1 mL
1/2 cup	firmly packed dark brown sugar	125 mL
2 cups	whole-wheat flour	500 mL

Microwave muffin pan, paper-lined

1. In a large bowl, combine Bran flakes and cooking bran. Add boiling water and stir to moisten evenly. Set aside to cool. Then add molasses, buttermilk, oil, browning sauce and dried fruit; blend together well.

2. In another bowl combine baking soda, baking powder, salt, sugar and flour. Add to bran mixture and stir just until moist.

3. Spoon batter into prepared muffin pan, filling cups two-thirds full. Bake on a rack for 2 1/2 to 3 minutes on High, rotating pan once during cooking time. Let stand for 3 to 5 minutes before removing muffins from pan.

HINT: For a special treat to keep kids happy while you're busy micro-baking, take simple chocolate or vanilla wafers and place a marshmallow on top of each. Microwave for 15 seconds. The marshmallows will fluff up to a fantastic size and the kids love it.

Vegetable Corn Muffins

1 cup	all-purpose flour	250 mL
1/2 cup	cornmeal	125 mL
1 tbsp	granulated sugar	15 mL
1 tbsp	baking powder	15 mL
1/2 tsp	salt	2 mL
3/4 tsp	Italian seasoning	4 mL
1/8 tsp	garlic powder	0.5 mL
2	eggs, beaten	2
1 tbsp	vegetable oil	15 mL
1/2 cup	drained corn kernels	125 mL
1/3 cup	milk (can use skim)	75 mL
1/3 cup	chopped green peppers	75 mL
1/4 cup	finely chopped onions	50 mL

Ramekins or microwave muffin pan, double paper-lined

1. In a large bowl, combine flour, cornmeal, sugar, baking powder, salt, Italian seasoning, garlic powder, eggs, oil, corn, milk, peppers and onions. Stir just until blended. Do not overmix.

2. Spoon batter into prepared ramekins or pan. Microwave on a rack on High for 2 1/2 to 3 minutes, rotating once halfway through cooking time. A toothpick inserted in the center of each muffin should come out clean and dry. Let stand for 3 to 5 minutes.

Whole-Wheat Honey Muffins

1 3/4 cups	whole-wheat flour	425 mL
4 tsp	baking powder	20 mL
1/2 tsp	salt	2 mL
1	egg, beaten	1
3/4 cup	milk	175 mL
1/3 cup	honey	75 mL
1/4 cup	vegetable oil	50 mL
1/3 cup	chopped walnuts	75 mL

Microwave muffin pan, paper-lined

1. In a large bowl, combine whole-wheat flour, baking powder and salt.

2. In another bowl, blend together egg, milk, honey, oil and walnuts.

3. Pour egg mixture into dry ingredients and stir until well moistened. The batter should be a bit lumpy.

4. Spoon batter into prepared pan, filling cups two-thirds full. (Baking may have to be done in batches.) Place muffin pan on a rack in the microwave. Bake on High for 2 1/2 minutes, rotating pan once during cooking. Let muffins stand for 3 to 5 minutes.

Special Yam Muffins

1 cup	all-purpose flour	250 mL
1/4 cup	granulated sugar	50 mL
1 tbsp	baking powder	15 mL
1 cup	yellow cornmeal	250 mL
1/2 tsp	salt	2 mL
1 1/4 tsp	cinnamon	6 mL
2	eggs	2
1/2 cup	cold strong coffee	125 mL
1/4 cup	butter or margarine, melted	50 mL
1/2 tsp	Tabasco sauce	2 mL
1 cup	mashed yams or sweet potatoes	250 mL

Ramekins or microwave muffin pan, double paper-lined

1. In a large bowl, combine flour, sugar, baking powder, cornmeal, salt and cinnamon. Make a well in the center.

2. In a medium bowl, beat eggs. Stir in coffee, butter, Tabasco sauce and yams. Add to flour mixture and stir just until moistened.

3. Spoon batter into prepared ramekins or pan, filling cups two-thirds full. (Baking may have to be done in batches.) If using ramekins, arrange in a circle. Microwave on High for 4 to 5 1/2 minutes, rotating pan or rearranging ramekins halfway through cooking time. A toothpick inserted in the center of each muffin should come out clean and dry. Let stand for 5 minutes. These muffins are delicious served warm.

Specially for Kids

Thiis chapter is specially written for kids. It contains recipes for muffins that kids will enjoy eating and making. The recipe on the opposite page is a basic, easy, plain muffin recipe — great for young cooks or anyone who has never baked muffins. The variations show you how to make a few changes and/or substitutions, and create a wide range of different flavored muffins. Following this recipe are other easy-to-make muffin recipes which I hope you will try to bake — and enjoy. When baking, keep the following tips in mind.

🧁 Make sure your oven racks are in the right position.

🧁 Set the oven to the temperature called for in your recipe so that the oven will be preheating and ready to use by the time you have mixed your muffin batter.

🧁 Grease your muffin tins, or line them with large-size paper baking cups and set aside.

🧁 In a large bowl, measure out all of your dry ingredients, for example, flour, sugar, baking powder, baking soda, salt, etc.

🧁 Make a well (hole) in the centre of these dry ingredients and set aside.

🧁 In a smaller bowl, combine your liquid ingredients, for example, milk, beaten eggs, oil, etc.

🧁 Add the smaller bowl of liquid ingredients all at once to the larger bowl of dry ingredients and stir only until the dry ingredients are just moistened. Do not overmix.

🧁 Spoon the batter into the tins, filling them three-quarters full, or fill the tins to the top for larger muffins.

🧁 Bake as directed in your recipe.

TO MEASURE DRY INGREDIENTS:

Use plastic or metal measuring cups that come in sets of different sizes. Spoon the dry ingredient into the right size cup until heaping, holding the cup over the canister it came in, or an empty bowl, not over the mixing bowl you are using to prepare the recipe.

Level the ingredient by scraping a knife across the top, allowing the excess amount to fall back into the canister or empty bowl. Do not tap the cup on the counter. Level measuring spoons containing a dry ingredient the same way.

TO MEASURE LIQUID INGREDIENTS:

To measure any liquid, use a measuring cup with a spout and amounts marked on the side of the cup. Place the cup on a counter and pour the liquid into the cup, bending down to read the measurements properly.

To measure small amounts, pour into measuring spoon until full, holding spoon away from your mixing bowl.

FRUITS AND VEGETABLES:

Always wash any fruits and vegetables before using them in your recipe.

Plain Muffins

2 cups	all-purpose flour	500 mL
3 tsp	baking powder	15 mL
1/4 cup	granulated sugar	50 mL
1/2 tsp	salt	2 mL
1 cup	milk	250 mL
1	egg, beaten	1
1/4 cup	vegetable oil	50 mL
1/2 tsp	vanilla	2 mL

Preheat oven to 400° F (200° C)
Muffin tin, greased or paper-lined

1. In a large bowl, combine flour, baking powder, sugar and salt. Make a well in the center.

2. In a smaller bowl, combine milk, beaten egg, oil and vanilla. Add liquid ingredients all at once to dry ingredients. Stir only until moistened and slightly lumpy.

3. Spoon batter into prepared muffin tin, filling cups three-quarters full. Bake in preheated oven for 20 to 25 minutes or until golden brown.

VARIATIONS

- **Orange Muffins:** Replace half or all of the milk with orange juice and add 1 tsp (5 mL) grated orange zest.

- **Cheese Muffins:** Reduce sugar to 2 tbsp (25 mL), add 1 cup (250 mL) grated cheese to the dry ingredients, and use 2 tbsp (25 mL) of oil instead of the 1/4 cup (50 mL).

- **Raisin Muffins:** Add 1/2 cup (125 mL) raisins to the dry ingredients.

- **Blueberry Muffins:** Fold in 1 cup (250 mL) fresh blueberries, or 3/4 cup (175 mL) thawed, well-drained frozen blueberries into the batter before spooning into the muffin tins.

HINT: If children (or adults) are sick in bed, serve their meals in a muffin tin. The cups hold assorted foods, even a small glass of milk or juice, and you will avoid sliding and spilling.

Once you feel confident in making plain muffins as in the recipe above, and adding different variations, you can start baking all kinds of delicious muffins using all kinds of ingredients. So, happy baking!

Apple Muffins

1 3/4 cups	all-purpose flour	425 mL
3 1/2 tsp	baking powder	17 mL
1/2 tsp	salt	2 mL
1/4 cup	granulated sugar	50 mL
1/2 tsp	ground nutmeg	2 mL
1 cup	milk	250 mL
1	egg, beaten	1
1/3 cup	vegetable oil	75 mL
1 tsp	grated lemon zest	5 mL
3/4 cup	shredded peeled apple	175 mL

Preheat oven to 400° F (200° C)
Muffin tin, greased or paper-lined

1. In a large bowl, combine flour, baking powder, salt, sugar and nutmeg. Make a well in the center.

2. In a small bowl, combine milk, beaten egg and oil. Add this mixture, all at once, to dry ingredients and stir just until moist. Fold in lemon zest and apple with just a few strokes. The batter will be a bit lumpy.

3. Spoon batter into prepared muffin tin, filling cups two-thirds full. Bake in preheated oven for 25 to 30 minutes.

Apple Cheddar Muffins

1/2 cup	butter *or* margarine	125 mL
1/2 cup	brown sugar	125 mL
2	eggs	2
1 2/3 cups	whole-wheat flour	410 mL
1/2 tsp	salt	2 mL
1 tsp	baking soda	5 mL
1/2 cup	rolled oats	125 mL
1 cup	apple pie filling	250 mL
1/2 cup	finely chopped, aged Cheddar cheese	125 mL
1/4 cup	milk *or* water	50 mL

Preheat oven to 400° F (200° C)
Muffin tin, greased or paper-lined

1. In a large bowl, cream together margarine and sugar. Add eggs and mix well. Add flour, salt and baking soda and mix. Add oats, pie filling and cheese and mix well. Stir in milk.

2. Spoon batter into prepared muffin tin, filling cups three-quarters full. Bake in preheated oven for 20 minutes.

VEGETABLE CORN MUFFINS (PAGE 27) ➤

Apple Honey Muffins

1 cup	applesauce	250 mL
1/3 cup	orange juice	75 mL
1/4 cup	honey	50 mL
1/4 cup	vegetable oil	50 mL
1	egg	1
1 cup	all-purpose flour	250 mL
3/4 cup	rolled oats	175 mL
1 tbsp	baking powder	15 mL
1/2 tsp	cinnamon	2 mL

Preheat oven to 400° F (200° C)
Muffin tin, greased or paper-lined

1. In a small bowl, mix together applesauce, orange juice, honey, oil and egg.

2. In a large bowl, mix together flour, rolled oats, baking powder and cinnamon. Make a well in the center.

3. Pour liquid ingredients into dry ingredients and stir just to moisten. Do not overmix. Spoon batter into prepared muffin tin. Bake in preheated oven for 25 to 30 minutes.

Apple Nut Muffins

2/3 cup	apple juice *or* milk	150 mL
1/2 cup	vegetable oil	125 mL
1 tsp	vanilla	5 mL
1	egg	1
2 cups	all-purpose flour	500 mL
1/4 cup	granulated sugar	50 mL
1/4 cup	firmly packed brown sugar	50 mL
1 tbsp	baking powder	15 mL
1/2 tsp	salt	2 mL
1/2 cup	chopped nuts	125 mL
1	chopped peeled apple	1
	SUGAR-CINNAMON MIX (see recipe, page 179)	

Preheat oven to 400° F (200° C)
Muffin tin, greased or paper-lined

1. In a large bowl, beat together juice, oil, vanilla and egg. Stir in flour, granulated sugar, brown sugar, baking powder and salt. Mix just until moistened. (Batter will be lumpy.) Stir in nuts and apple.

2. Spoon batter into prepared muffin tin, filling cups three-quarters full. Sprinkle with SUGAR-CINNAMON MIX. Bake in preheated oven for 20 minutes or until golden brown.

HINT: To soften rock-hard brown sugar, put a piece of cut apple in the container. Leave for one day, remove, and fluff up the sugar with a fork.

◄ "CANDY APPLE" MUFFINS (PAGE 47)

Special Banana Muffins

1 cup	granulated sugar	250 mL
2	eggs	2
1/2 cup	softened margarine	125 mL
2 cups	all-purpose flour	500 mL
2 tsp	baking soda	10 mL
3	medium bananas, mashed	3

Preheat oven to 425 ° F (220° C)
Muffin tin, paper-lined

1. In a large bowl, cream together sugar and eggs until well mixed. Add margarine and blend well. Add flour and baking soda and blend until mixture resembles a loose dough. Add bananas and stir just until moist and blended.

2. Spoon batter into prepared muffin tin, filling cups to the top. Bake in preheated oven for 15 to 20 minutes or until golden brown.

Banana Split Muffins

2	egg whites	2
1/3 cup	granulated sugar	75 mL
2/3 cup	flaked coconut	150 mL
2 cups	packaged biscuit mix	500 mL
1/4 cup	granulated sugar	50 mL
2/3 cup	milk	150 mL
2 tbsp	shortening, melted	25 mL
2	egg yolks, beaten	2
Half	small banana, cut into 12 cubes	Half
12	maraschino cherries, halved	12
12	walnut halves	12

Preheat oven to 400° F (200° C)
12-cup muffin tin, greased or paper-lined

1. In a small bowl, beat egg whites until soft peaks form. Gradually add 1/3 cup (75 mL) sugar and continue beating until stiff peaks form. Fold in coconut and set aside.

2. In a large bowl, mix together biscuit mix and 1/4 cup (50 mL) sugar.

3. In another bowl, combine milk, shortening and egg yolks. Add this mixture all at once to dry ingredients. Stir just until moistened.

4. Spoon 1 1/2 tbsp (20 mL) batter into the bottom of each prepared cup. Place a banana cube, cherry half and walnut half on top of batter. Cover with 1 tbsp (15 mL) more batter. Spoon 1 1/2 tbsp (20 mL) meringue mixture on each muffin. Top with remaining cherries. Bake in preheated oven for 15 to 20 minutes.

Banana Walnut Muffins

1 1/2 cups	all-purpose flour	375 mL
3/4 cup	granulated sugar	175 mL
3/4 cup	chopped walnuts (about 3 oz [75 g])	175 mL
1 1/2 tsp	baking soda	7 mL
1/4 tsp	salt	1 mL
1 1/4 cups	mashed ripe bananas	300 mL
1/2 cup	melted unsalted butter (1 stick)	125 mL
1	egg	1
2 1/2 tbsp	milk	35 mL

Preheat oven to 350° F (180° C)
Muffin tin, greased or paper-lined

1. In a large bowl, combine flour, sugar, chopped walnuts, baking soda and salt.

2. In another bowl, combine mashed bananas, melted butter, egg and milk. Add to dry ingredients and stir just until moistened. Do not overmix.

3. Spoon batter into prepared muffin tin, filling cups three-quarters full. Bake in preheated oven for 25 minutes or until a toothpick inserted in center of muffin comes out dry.

HINT: For a nice thick milkshake to enjoy with your muffins, put half a banana, 1/2 cup (125 mL) each of 2% milk, plain yogurt and sliced strawberries (or blueberries) in a blender and purée.

Barbecue Muffins

1	pkg (10 oz [284 mL]) refrigerated buttermilk biscuits	1
1/2 cup	tomato ketchup	125 mL
3 tbsp	packed brown sugar	45 mL
1 tbsp	cider vinegar	15 mL
1/2 tsp	chili powder	2 mL
1 lb	ground beef	500 g
1 cup	shredded Cheddar cheese	250 mL

Preheat oven to 375° F (190° C)
Muffin tin, greased

1. Remove dough from package and separate into 10 biscuits. With the palm of your hand or a small rolling pin, flatten each biscuit into 5-inch (12.5 cm) circles. Press dough into the bottom and up the sides of each prepared cup. Set aside.

2. In a small bowl, combine ketchup, brown sugar, vinegar and chili powder, stirring until smooth.

3. In a skillet over medium-high heat, brown the ground beef. Drain the fat and add ketchup mixture, mixing well.

4. Divide meat equally among the biscuit-lined muffin cups, about 1/4 cup (50 mL) each. Sprinkle with cheese. Bake in preheated oven for 20 minutes or until golden brown. Allow to cool before serving.

Blueberry Breakfast Gems

2 cups	all-purpose flour	500 mL
3 tbsp	packed brown sugar	45 mL
1 tbsp	baking powder	15 mL
1/2 tsp	salt	2 mL
1 cup	milk	250 mL
1	egg	1
1/4 cup	butter or margarine, melted	50 mL
1 cup	fresh blueberries (or frozen)	250 mL
2 tbsp	granulated sugar	25 mL

Preheat oven to 425° F (220° C)
Muffin tin, greased or paper-lined

1. In a large bowl, mix together flour, brown sugar, baking powder and salt.

2. In a small bowl, combine milk, egg, and butter; mix until well blended. Add to the flour mixture and stir just until moistened. Do not overmix. Fold in the blueberries.

3. Spoon batter into prepared muffin tin. Sprinkle sugar over tops. Bake in preheated oven for 20 to 25 minutes or until golden brown.

Blueberry Cheese Muffins

1 1/2 cups	all-purpose flour	375 mL
1/4 cup	granulated sugar	50 mL
3 tsp	baking powder	15 mL
1 tsp	salt	5 mL
1 cup	yellow cornmeal	250 mL
2 cups	grated sharp Cheddar cheese	500 mL
2 cups	fresh blueberries, rinsed and drained	500 mL
1 cup	milk	250 mL
1	egg, beaten	1
1/4 cup	butter or margarine, melted	50 mL

Preheat oven to 400° F (200° C)
Muffin tin, greased or paper-lined

1. In a large bowl, mix together flour, sugar, baking powder, salt, cornmeal, cheese and blueberries.

2. In another bowl, beat together milk, egg and melted butter. Add all at once to the flour mixture, stirring just until blended.

3. Spoon batter into prepared muffin tin, filling cups three-quarters full. Bake in preheated oven for 20 to 25 minutes.

Blueberry Cornmeal Muffins

1 cup	all-purpose flour	250 mL
1 cup	yellow cornmeal	250 mL
1/4 cup	granulated sugar	50 mL
1 tsp	baking soda	5 mL
1 tsp	baking powder	5 mL
1/2 tsp	salt	2 mL
2 tsp	finely grated lemon zest	10 mL
1 1/2 cups	buttermilk	375 mL
1	egg	1
1/4 cup	butter or margarine, melted	50 mL
1 tsp	vanilla	5 mL
1 1/2 cups	fresh blueberries (or frozen)	375 mL

Preheat oven to 400° F (200° C)
Muffin tin, greased or paper-lined

1. In a large bowl, combine flour, cornmeal, sugar, baking soda, baking powder, salt and lemon zest.

2. In another bowl, whisk together buttermilk, egg, butter and vanilla. Pour into flour mixture and stir just until moistened. Do not overmix. Fold in blueberries.

3. Spoon batter into prepared muffin tin, filling cups three-quarters full. Bake in preheated oven for 20 to 25 minutes or until golden brown.

Easy Blueberry Muffins

1 3/4 cups	all-purpose flour	425 mL
1/3 cup	granulated sugar	75 mL
3 tsp	baking powder	15 mL
3/4 tsp	salt	4 mL
3/4 cup	milk	175 mL
1/3 cup	vegetable oil	75 mL
1	egg	1
1 cup	fresh blueberries (or thawed and drained frozen blueberries)	250 mL

Preheat oven to 400° F (200° C)
Muffin tin, greased or paper-lined

1. In a large bowl, mix together flour, sugar, baking powder and salt until blended.

2. In another bowl, beat together milk, oil and egg. Add to the flour mixture and stir only until moistened. Do not overmix. Gently fold in blueberries.

3. Spoon batter into prepared muffin tin, filling cups three-quarters full. Bake in preheated oven for 20 to 25 minutes. Delicious served warm.

HINT: When your friends come over to visit, if their parents (or your parents) want them sent home at a certain time, set the kitchen timer — just as you do in baking. When the buzzer sounds, home they go. Moms will be happy.

More Blueberry Muffins

2 cups	all-purpose flour	500 mL
2 tsp	baking powder	10 mL
1/4 tsp	salt	1 mL
1/2 cup	softened butter	125 mL
1 cup	granulated sugar	250 mL
2	eggs	2
3/4 cup	milk	175 mL
1 1/2 cups	blueberries	375 mL

Preheat oven to 375° F (190° C)
Muffin tin, greased or paper-lined

1. In a large bowl, mix together flour, baking powder and salt. Make a well in the center.

2. In another bowl, cream together butter and sugar, then beat in eggs one at a time. Gradually stir in milk. The mixture may look curdled. Pour into the flour mixture and stir just until moistened. Gently fold in blueberries.

3. Spoon batter into prepared muffin tin, filling cups to the top. Bake in preheated oven for 25 to 30 minutes or until toothpick inserted in center of a muffin comes out clean and dry.

Blueberry Oat Muffins

1 cup	quick-cooking rolled oats	250 mL
1 cup	water	250 mL
1 cup + 3 tbsp	oat bran cereal	250 mL + 45 mL
1 tsp	baking powder	5 mL
1/2 tsp	baking soda	2 mL
1/2 tsp	sea salt	2 mL
3/4 cup	packed brown sugar	175 mL
1	egg, beaten	1
1/4 cup	vegetable oil	50 mL
1 1/4 cups	fresh or frozen blueberries	300 mL

Preheat oven to 400° F (200° C)
Muffin tin, greased or paper-lined

1. In a medium bowl, combine quick-cooking oats and water. Set aside.

2. In a large bowl, mix together oat bran cereal, baking powder, baking soda, sea salt and brown sugar Add egg and oil and mix only until blended. Add the oats and mix only until blended. Fold in blueberries and stir only until moistened. Do not overmix.

3. Spoon batter into prepared muffin tin, filling cups three-quarters or to the top. Bake in preheated oven for 20 to 25 minutes or until done.

Blueberry Orange Muffins

2 cups	all-purpose flour	500 mL
1 tbsp	baking powder	15 mL
1/2 tsp	cinnamon	2 mL
1/2 cup	vegetable oil	125 mL
2	eggs	2
1/3 cup	honey	75 mL
1/4 cup	milk	50 mL
1/4 cup	orange juice	50 mL
1 1/2 cups	fresh blueberries	375 mL

Preheat oven to 400° F (200° C)
Muffin tin, paper-lined

1. In a large bowl, combine flour, baking powder and cinnamon. Make a well in the center.

2. In another bowl, beat together oil, eggs, honey, milk and orange juice. Pour into flour mixture and blend just until moistened. Fold in blueberries.

3. Spoon batter into prepared muffin tin, filling cups three-quarters full. Bake in preheated oven for 20 to 25 minutes or until golden brown.

Bran Cereal Muffins

1 1/4 cups	all-purpose flour	300 mL
3 tsp	baking powder	15 mL
1/2 tsp	salt	2 mL
1/2 cup	granulated sugar	125 mL
1 1/2 cups	All-Bran cereal	375 mL
1 1/4 cups	milk	300 mL
1	egg	1
1/3 cup	vegetable oil	75 mL

Preheat oven to 400° F (200° C)
12-cup muffin tin, paper-lined

1. In a large bowl, mix together flour, baking powder, salt and sugar. Set aside.

2. In another bowl combine cereal and milk. Stir well and let stand for 1 to 2 minutes or until the cereal has softened. Add the egg and oil to this cereal mixture and beat well. Pour into the flour mixture and stir just until moistened.

3. Spoon batter evenly into prepared muffin tin. Bake in preheated oven for 25 minutes or until lightly browned.

VARIATIONS

🧁 Add 1/2 cup (125 mL) raisins to the batter.

🧁 Substitute 3 cups (750 mL) Raisin Bran cereal, or 2 1/2 cups (625 mL) Bran Flakes cereal in place of the All-Bran cereal.

Quick Breakfast Muffins

2 cups	all-purpose flour	500 mL
4 tsp	baking powder	20 mL
4 tbsp	granulated sugar	50 mL
Pinch	salt	Pinch
1	egg	1
1 cup	milk	250 mL
2 tbsp	vegetable oil *or* melted butter	25 mL

Preheat oven to 375° F (190° C)
Muffin tin, paper-lined

1. In a large bowl, mix together flour, baking powder, sugar and salt. Make a well in the center.

2. In another bowl, whisk together egg, milk and oil. Pour into dry ingredients and stir only until moistened. Do not overmix.

3. Spoon batter into prepared muffin tin, filling cups to the top. Bake in preheated oven for 20 to 25 minutes or until done.

NOTE: If you want to save time in the morning, mix the dry ingredients the night before, cover and set aside on the counter. Blend together the liquid ingredients and set aside in the fridge until the morning. Then, all you have to do for a really quick breakfast muffin is pour the liquid ingredients into the dry ingredients and bake as above.

Chili Muffins

1 lb	lean ground beef	500 g
3/4 cup	salsa (medium)	175 mL
1 tsp	chili powder	5 mL
1/2 tsp	salt	2 mL
1/4 tsp	pepper	1 mL
1	can (14 oz [398 mL]) red kidney beans, rinsed and drained	1
1/2 cup	shredded Cheddar cheese (or Monterey Jack, etc.)	125 mL

Preheat oven to 400° F (200° C)
8-cup muffin tin

1. In a large bowl, break up the beef with a fork. Mix in 1/4 cup (50 mL) of the salsa, chili powder, salt and pepper. Divide evenly into 8 muffin cups. Press into the center of each to form a well and press into the bottom and up sides of each cup. Bake in preheated oven for 10 minutes or until the meat is no longer pink.

2. In another bowl, combine beans and remaining salsa. Spoon into the muffin cups. Sprinkle with cheese. Bake for 7 or 8 minutes or until the beans are hot and the cheese is melted.

HINT: Make mini meat loaves by patting meat mixture into muffin pan cups. Brush each generously with barbecue sauce and bake.

Who doesn't love chocolate? On Friday — "treat day" in our house — these are at the top of the list.

Chocolate Muffins

1 2/3 cups	all-purpose flour	400 mL
3/4 cup	granulated sugar	175 mL
1/3 cup	cocoa	75 mL
3 1/2 tsp	baking powder	17 mL
1/2 tsp	salt	2 mL
1	egg	1
1 cup	milk	250 mL
1/4 cup	vegetable oil *or* shortening, melted	50 mL

Preheat oven to 400° F (200° C)
Muffin tin, greased or paper-lined

1. In a large bowl, combine flour, sugar, cocoa, baking powder and salt.

2. In another bowl, beat together egg, milk and oil. Pour into the flour mixture and stir just until combined. Do not overmix.

3. Spoon batter into prepared muffin tin, filling cups three-quarters full. Bake in preheated oven for 20 to 25 minutes.

VARIATION

Chocolate Nut Muffins: Add 1/2 cup (125 mL) chopped walnuts to the batter and bake as above.

Chocolate Chip Muffins

1	egg	1
1 cup	sour cream	250 mL
1/2 cup	milk	125 mL
1 3/4 cups	all-purpose flour	425 mL
2 tbsp	granulated sugar	25 mL
1 tsp	baking powder	5 mL
1/2 tsp	baking soda	2 mL
1 tsp	salt	5 mL
1 cup	chocolate chips	250 mL

Preheat oven to 400° F (200° C)
Muffin tin, greased or paper-lined

1. In a bowl, beat egg. Stir in sour cream and milk.

2. In a large bowl, combine flour, sugar, baking powder, baking soda and salt. Pour egg mixture into flour mixture and stir just until moistened. Fold in chocolate chips.

3. Spoon batter into prepared muffin tin, filling cups three-quarters full. Bake in preheated oven for 20 to 25 minutes.

Chocolate Chip Banana Muffins

2	ripe bananas	2
1 tsp	baking soda	5 mL
1 tsp	hot water	5 mL
1/2 cup	margarine *or* vegetable oil	125 mL
3/4 cup	granulated sugar	175 mL
1	egg, beaten	1
1 tsp	vanilla	5 mL
1 1/2 cups	all-purpose flour	375 mL
1 tsp	baking powder	5 mL
1 tsp	salt	5 mL
5 oz	chocolate chips	150 g

Preheat oven to 425° F (220° C)
Muffin tin, greased or paper-lined

1. In a medium bowl, mash bananas. Add baking soda and hot water and set aside.

2. In a large bowl, cream together margarine and sugar. Add egg and vanilla; mix well. Add flour, baking powder and salt. Add banana mixture and blend together. Add chocolate chips; stir just until moistened.

3. Spoon batter into prepared muffin tin. Bake in preheated oven for 15 to 20 minutes.

Chocolate Chunk Banana Muffins

This recipe contains a surprise ingredient, Miracle Whip, and it's delicious.

1 cup	mashed overripe bananas (about 2 medium)	250 mL
1 cup	low-fat Miracle Whip	250 mL
1/2 cup	granulated sugar	125 mL
1/2 tsp	vanilla	2 mL
2 cups	all-purpose flour	500 mL
2 tsp	baking soda	10 mL
1/2 cup	chocolate chunks (or cut up a plain chocolate bar)	125 mL

Preheat oven to 375° F (190° C)
Muffin tin, greased or paper-lined

1. In a large bowl, combine bananas, Miracle Whip, sugar and vanilla.

2. In another bowl, whisk together flour and baking soda. Fold into the banana mixture and stir just until blended. Fold in chocolate chunks.

3. Spoon batter into prepared muffin tin. Bake in preheated oven for 20 minutes or until golden brown.

NOTE: You could use chocolate chips in place of the chocolate chunks. Using the Miracle Whip means you don't have to add an egg to this recipe, and the muffins are nice and moist.

Chocolate Lovers' Delight

3	squares unsweetened chocolate	3
1/3 cup	vegetable oil	75 mL
2	eggs	2
1 tsp	vanilla	5 mL
1 1/3 cups	milk	325 mL
2 cups	all-purpose flour	500 mL
1/2 cup	granulated sugar	125 mL
2 tsp	baking soda	10 mL
1 cup	semi-sweet chocolate chips	250 mL

Preheat oven to 400° F (200° C)
Muffin tin, paper-lined

1. In a saucepan over low heat, melt the chocolate with the oil (or microwave on Medium for 2 minutes). Remove from heat and add eggs, vanilla and milk; blend well.

2. In a large bowl, combine flour, sugar and baking soda. Add the chocolate mixture and half the chocolate chips, stirring only until moistened.

3. Spoon batter into prepared muffin tin, filling cups two-thirds full. Sprinkle with remaining chocolate chips. Bake in preheated oven for 20 to 25 minutes or until a toothpick inserted in the center comes out clean.

HINT: An ice-cream scoop makes filling muffin cups a breeze. To make muffins mushroom out, use an oiled scoop.

Great with ice-cream!

Double Chocolate Muffins

1 cup	semi-sweet chocolate chips	250 mL
1 tbsp	instant coffee crystals	15 mL
1/4 cup	margarine	50 mL
1 1/4 cups	milk	300 mL
1	egg	1
2 1/2 cups	all-purpose flour	625 mL
1/3 cup	granulated sugar	75 mL
1 tbsp	baking powder	15 mL
1/2 tsp	salt	2 mL

Preheat oven to 400° F (200° C)
Muffin tin, paper-lined

1. In a saucepan over low heat, melt 1/2 cup (125 mL) of the chocolate chips, coffee, margarine and milk, stirring to blend well. Set aside. When mixture cools, beat in egg.

2. In a large bowl, combine flour, sugar, baking powder and salt. Stir in chocolate mixture, stirring just until moistened. Fold in the remaining 1/2 cup (125 mL) chocolate chips.

3. Spoon batter into prepared muffin tin, filling cups to the top. Bake in preheated oven for 20 minutes or until a toothpick inserted in center of a muffin comes out clean and dry.

HINT: To avoid the mess of serving ice-cream at children's parties, prepare the ice-cream in balls. Put them into muffin tins and store in freezer until it is time to serve them. This makes dishing it out easier and faster and avoids the usual "he/she got more than I did!"

Peanut Butter Cornmeal Muffins

1 cup	all-purpose flour	250 mL
1/2 tsp	salt	2 mL
3 tsp	baking powder	15 mL
1 tbsp	granulated sugar	15 mL
1/2 cup	cornmeal	125 mL
1 cup	milk	250 mL
1	egg, beaten	1
1/4 cup	peanut butter	50 mL
1 tbsp	butter or shortening, melted	15 mL

Preheat oven to 400° F (200° C)
Muffin tin, greased or paper-lined

1. In a large bowl, combine flour, salt, baking powder and sugar. Stir in cornmeal.

2. In another bowl, combine milk, egg, peanut butter and melted butter. Add the milk mixture, stirring only until moistened. Do not overmix.

3. Spoon batter into prepared muffin tin, filling cups three-quarters full. Bake in preheated oven for 20 to 25 minutes or until done.

Surprise Cornmeal Muffins

1 cup	yellow cornmeal	250 mL
1 1/4 cups	cake-and-pastry flour	300 mL
1 tsp	baking soda	5 mL
2 tsp	baking powder	10 mL
1/2 tsp	salt	2 mL
1/2 cup	shortening *or* butter	125 mL
1/2 cup	granulated sugar	125 mL
1	egg	1
1 cup	milk	250 mL
1/2 cup	plain yogurt	125 mL
1/4 cup	filling (such as softened cream cheese, jam etc.)	50 mL

Preheat oven to 400° F (200° C)
12-cup muffin tin, paper-lined

1. In a large bowl, combine cornmeal, flour, baking soda, baking powder and salt.

2. In another bowl, cream together shortening and sugar. Beat in egg, milk and yogurt. Pour into dry ingredients and stir just until moistened.

3. Spoon half the batter evenly into prepared muffin tin. Top each with 1 tsp (5 mL) filling and then spoon remaining batter evenly over top. Bake in preheated oven for 20 to 25 minutes or until golden brown.

Have Mom show you how to cut off the kernels of corn from cooked corn-on-the-cob, or you can use frozen or canned kernel corn.

1 cup	all-purpose flour	250 mL
3/4 cup	yellow cornmeal	175 mL
2 tbsp	granulated sugar	25 mL
2 tsp	baking powder	10 mL
3/4 tsp	salt	4 mL
1	egg, beaten	1
3/4 cup	milk	175 mL
1/4 cup	butter or margarine, melted	50 mL
1/2 cup	cooked corn, cut off the cob	125 mL
2 tbsp	minced green onion (optional)	25 mL

Corn-on-the-Cob Muffins

Preheat oven to 425° F (220° C)
Muffin tin, paper-lined

1. In a large bowl, combine flour, cornmeal, sugar, baking powder and salt.

2. In a small bowl, combine egg, milk, butter, corn and onion. Pour into dry ingredients and stir just until moistened and blended.

3. Spoon batter into prepared muffin tin. Bake in preheated oven for 20 minutes or until lightly browned.

HINT: Top hot, baked muffins (or cupcakes) with a marshmallow and put back in oven until marshmallows melt and brown lightly.

You're the boss for these muffins. Feel free to add whatever you like. I like salt, pepper, fresh herbs, onions, tomatoes and green peppers. Be imaginative!

1	loaf of bread (white or brown)	1
	Cheddar cheese slices, about 1/2 inch (1 cm) thick	
	Eggs	
	Toppings (see above)	

Egg Bread Muffins

Preheat oven to 350° F (180° C)
Muffin tin, greased

1. Arrange bread slices on a cutting board. Cut out circles the same size as bottom of muffin tin cups, using a cookie cutter or top of a glass. Make as many as you want.

2. Place circles of bread in bottom of each prepared muffin cup. Place cheese slices on top of each bread circle. Break an egg over top. Add your choice of toppings.

3. Bake in preheated oven until tops turn golden brown or longer if you want a firmer yolk. Serve immediately.

Fudgey Nut Muffins

1 cup	all-purpose flour	250 mL
1 1/3 cups	granulated sugar	325 mL
1 1/4 tsp	baking powder	6 mL
1/2 tsp	salt	2 mL
1/4 tsp	baking soda	1 mL
1 cup	milk	250 mL
3 tbsp	butter or shortening, melted	45 mL
1	egg	1
1/2 tsp	vanilla	2 mL
3	squares unsweetened chocolate, melted and cooled	3
1	pkg (6 oz [175 g]) semi-sweet chocolate chips	1
1/2 cup	chopped walnuts	125 mL

Preheat oven to 400° F (200° C)
Muffin tin, greased or paper-lined

1. In a large bowl, combine flour, sugar, baking powder, salt and baking soda. Make a well in the center. Add milk, butter, egg, vanilla and melted chocolate; stir just until moistened and blended. Fold in the chocolate chips and walnuts.

2. Spoon batter into prepared muffin tin, filling cups three-quarters full or to the top if a larger muffin is desired. Bake in preheated oven for 20 to 25 minutes or until toothpick inserted in center of a muffin comes out clean and dry.

HINT: Hey kids! Get Mom to buy your favorite cake mix. Prepare the batter as directed on the package. Use flat-bottomed ice-cream cones. Fill one-quarter full with the batter. Bake at 375° F (190° C.) for 20 minutes or until done. Frost and decorate with chocolate chips, miniature marshmallows, candy, raisins or whatever you happen to have on hand.

This recipe uses English muffins, which are completely different from regular muffins. You can buy them in most bakery sections in supermarkets. If you can't find any, you can use scones instead.

Funny Face Tuna Melts

1	can (6.5 oz [184 g]) flaked tuna, drained	1
2 tbsp	mayonnaise	25 mL
1	celery stalk, chopped	1
1/4 cup	grated Cheddar cheese	50 mL
	Black pepper	
2 or 3	English Muffins, split in half	2 or 3
	Pickle slices	
	Olives	
	Tomato slices	

1. In a bowl combine tuna, mayonnaise, celery, cheese and pepper to taste. Divide mixture evenly over each muffin half.

2. Make "funny faces" on each half, using pickle slices for eyes, olives for the nose and half a tomato slice for smiling mouths. Use any other garnishes you have on hand as well. Place under the broiler for 3 to 5 minutes or until cheese melts.

NOTE: In place of the tuna, try canned salmon, turkey or chicken, or mashed hard-boiled eggs. You might also try using green or red bell peppers, raisins, mushrooms, or anything else you like to make the "funny faces."

"Candy Apple" Muffins

Your muffins will look like real taffy-candied apples.

2 cups	all-purpose flour	500 mL
1/2 cup	granulated sugar	125 mL
1 tbsp	baking powder	15 mL
1/2 tsp	salt	2 mL
1/4 tsp	ground nutmeg	1 mL
1/2 cup	milk	125 mL
1/4 cup	butter or margarine, melted	50 mL
2	eggs	2
1 tsp	vanilla	5 mL
1	apple, chopped	1
DIP		
1/2 cup	honey	125 mL
1/2 cup	packed dark brown sugar	125 mL
3/4 cup	finely chopped walnuts	175 mL

Preheat oven to 400° F (200° C)
Muffin tin, greased
Wooden skewers or popsicle sticks

1. In a large bowl, mix together flour, sugar, baking powder, salt and nutmeg.

2. In another bowl, combine milk, butter, eggs and vanilla until well blended. Pour into dry ingredients and stir until just moistened. Fold in apple. Do not overmix.

3. Spoon batter into prepared muffin tin, filling cups two-thirds full. Bake in preheated oven for 15 to 20 minutes or until lightly browned. Cool slightly and remove from pan.

4. In a saucepan over medium heat, bring honey and brown sugar to a boil. Stir until sugar is dissolved. Pour walnuts onto a plate.

5. Spear warm muffins with a skewer or popsicle stick and dip quickly into the honey/brown sugar mixture, then into chopped nuts.

NOTE: You can use a miniature muffin tin and bake for 12 to 15 minutes.

HINT: Put medium-sized apples into muffin tins. Bake as in any baked apple recipe.

Halloween Monster Muffins

1 1/2 cups	all-purpose flour	375 mL
2 tsp	baking powder	10 mL
1/2 tsp	salt	2 mL
1 tsp	cinnamon	5 mL
1/2 tsp	ground ginger	2 mL
1/4 tsp	ground cloves	1 mL
1/4 tsp	ground nutmeg	1 mL
1/2 cup	packed brown sugar	125 mL
1/2 cup	raisins (optional)	125 mL
1	egg	1
1/2 cup	milk	125 mL
1/2 cup	canned pumpkin purée	125 mL
1/4 cup	vegetable oil	50 mL

Preheat oven to 400° F (200° C)
Muffin tin, paper-lined

1. In a large bowl, combine flour, baking powder, salt, cinnamon, ginger, cloves, nutmeg and brown sugar. Mix in raisins, if using. Make a well in the center.

2. In a smaller bowl, beat together egg, milk, pumpkin and oil. Pour into flour mixture and stir just until moistened. The batter will be lumpy.

3. Spoon batter into prepared muffin tin. Bake in preheated oven for about 20 minutes.

4. Decorate with vanilla or cream-cheese frosting or whipping cream. Use raisins, chipits, smarties, carrot or green bell pepper pieces, nuts, or whatever else you have on hand to make all kinds of scary monster faces on your muffin tops.

Ham And Cheddar Muffins

2 cups	biscuit mix	500 mL
2 tsp	dry mustard	10 mL
1	egg, beaten	1
1/2 cup	milk	125 mL
1	can (6.5 oz [184 g]) flaked ham, flaked with a fork	1
1 1/2 cups	grated Cheddar cheese	375 mL

Preheat oven to 400° F (200° C)
Muffin tin, greased or paper-lined

1. In a medium bowl, combine biscuit mix, mustard, egg and milk with a fork. Stir in flaked ham and cheese just until moistened.

2. Spoon batter into prepared muffin tin, filling cups three-quarters full. Bake in preheated oven for 20 to 25 minutes or until done.

VARIATION

☕ If you want a sweet muffin instead, use 2 tbsp (25 mL) sugar in place of the dry mustard.

Hamburger Muffins

18	slices white or brown bread	18
	Butter	
1 lb	lean ground beef	500 g
1 cup	canned mushroom soup	250 mL
1/4 cup	chopped onions	50 mL
1	egg, beaten	1
1/2 cup	grated Cheddar cheese	125 mL
1 tsp	Worcestershire sauce	5 mL
	Salt and pepper, to taste	

Preheat oven to 350° F (180° C)
Muffin tin

1. Trim the crusts off bread slices and flatten slightly with a rolling pin. Butter each slice on one side and place, buttered-side down, in muffin cups. Set aside.

2. In a bowl mix together meat, soup, onions, egg, cheese, Worcestershire sauce, salt and pepper. Spoon mixture evenly over bread slices. Bake in preheated oven for 35 to 45 minutes or until meat is well-cooked.

Hot Chocolate Puddings with Marshmallow Topping

Here's a great treat using custard cups instead of muffin tins.

1	pkg chocolate pudding and pie filling	1
2 cups	miniature marshmallows	500 mL

Six 6-oz (175 g) ramekins

1. Prepare pudding as directed on package. Remove from heat and stir in 1 1/2 cups (375 mL) of the marshmallows just until mixed, not melted. Pour into ramekins. Top with remaining marshmallows. Serve hot.

Jam-Filled Muffins

1 3/4 cups	all-purpose flour	425 mL
1/2 cup	granulated sugar	125 mL
1 tbsp	baking powder	15 mL
1/2 tsp	salt	2 mL
2	eggs	2
2/3 cup	milk	150 mL
1/3 cup	butter or margarine, melted	75 mL
1 tsp	grated lemon zest	5 mL
1/2 cup	strawberry or raspberry jam	125 mL

Preheat oven to 400° F (200° C)
12-cup muffin tin, greased or paper-lined

1. In a large bowl, mix together flour, sugar, baking powder and salt.

2. In another bowl, lightly beat eggs. Add milk, butter and lemon zest. Pour into flour mixture, stirring just until moistened and blended. Do not overmix.

3. Spoon half the batter into prepared muffin tin. Make a well in the center of each cup and add a spoonful of jam. Spoon remaining batter over jam. Bake in preheated oven for 20 to 25 minutes or until golden brown.

Here is another recipe using English Muffins.

Little Miss Muffins

1	can (6.5 oz [184 g]) flaked chicken or tuna, well-drained	1
1/4 cup	mayonnaise	50 mL
1	tomato, peeled, seeded and chopped	1
1 tbsp	lemon juice	15 mL
	Salt and pepper to taste	
	Butter	
2	English muffins, split and toasted	2
1	small cucumber, scored and sliced	1
2	slices processed cheese, each cut diagonally in half	2
1	tomato, sliced	1

1. In a bowl mix together chicken, mayonnaise, chopped tomato, lemon juice, salt and pepper.

2. Butter the toasted English muffins and put cucumber slices and chicken mixture on each half. Top with cheese and tomato slices. Broil for 2 to 3 minutes or until cheese melts.

HINT: To peel a tomato, lower the tomato into boiling water for 5 seconds. Remove from water and the peel should come off easily. If not, repeat and try again.

Meal in a Muffin

8 oz	boiled ham, cut into chunks	250 g
1 1/2	slices rye bread, crusts removed and torn into pieces	1 1/2
2 tbsp	minced green onion	25 mL
2 tbsp	fresh parsley	25 mL
1	egg yolk	1
1 tbsp	unsweetened apricot jam	15 mL
1 tsp	honey mustard	5 mL

Preheat oven to 350° F (180° C)
6-cup muffin tin

1. In a food processor, combine ham, bread, onion, parsley, egg yolk and jam; process until ground.

2. Spoon mixture evenly into muffin cups. Bake in preheated oven for 30 minutes. Remove from oven and brush tops with mustard. Return to oven and bake for 5 more minutes. Remove from cups and cool just enough to eat.

Oatmeal Cinnamon Muffins

1 cup	all-purpose flour	250 mL
3 1/2 tsp	baking powder	17 mL
1/2 tsp	salt	2 mL
1/2 tsp	cinnamon	2 mL
Pinch	ground nutmeg	Pinch
3/4 cup	rolled oats	175 mL
1/2 cup	lightly packed brown sugar	125 mL
1	egg	1
1 cup	milk	250 mL
1/4 cup	vegetable oil *or* shortening, melted	50 mL

Preheat oven to 400° F (200° C)
Muffin tin, greased or paper-lined

1. In a large bowl, combine flour, baking powder, salt, cinnamon and nutmeg. Stir in rolled oats and brown sugar; blend together well.

2. In another bowl, beat together egg, milk and oil. Add to flour mixture and stir only until moistened. Batter will be lumpy.

3. Spoon batter into prepared muffin tin, filling cups two-thirds full. Bake in preheated oven for 20 to 25 minutes or until done.

Miniature Orange Muffins

Makes about 36 miniature, bite-sized muffins.

2 cups	all-purpose flour	500 mL
1 tsp	baking soda	5 mL
1 tsp	salt	5 mL
1 tsp	grated orange zest	5 mL
1/2 cup	butter, at room temperature	125 mL
1 cup	granulated sugar	250 mL
3/4 cup	sour cream	175 mL
1/2 cup	raisins	125 mL
1/2 cup	chopped nuts	125 mL
Dip		
1 cup	granulated sugar	250 mL
1/2 cup	orange juice (juice of 1 orange)	125 mL

Preheat oven to 375° F (190° C)
Miniature muffin tin, greased

1. In a large bowl, combine flour, baking soda, salt and zest.

2. In another bowl, cream together butter and the 1 cup (250 mL) sugar. Add sour cream alternately with flour mixture, stirring just until moistened and blended. Fold in raisins and nuts.

3. Spoon batter into prepared muffin tin, filling cups to the top. Bake in preheated oven for 12 to 15 minutes.

4. In a small bowl, mix together sugar and orange juice. Dip warm muffins into dip mixture. Let cool before serving.

Orange Raisin Muffins

2 cups	all-purpose flour	500 mL
1/3 cup	granulated sugar	75 mL
1/2 tsp	salt	2 mL
3/4 tsp	baking soda	4 mL
1/2 cup	raisins	125 mL
1	egg, well-beaten	1
1/3 cup	orange juice	75 mL
1/2 tsp	grated orange zest	2 mL
2/3 cup	buttermilk *or* sour milk	150 mL
1/3 cup	shortening	75 mL

Preheat oven to 425° F (220° C)
Muffin tin, greased

1. In a large bowl, mix together flour, sugar, salt and baking soda. Add raisins.

2. In a smaller bowl, combine beaten egg, orange juice, zest, buttermilk and shortening. Pour into dry ingredients and stir just until moistened and blended.

3. Spoon batter into prepared muffin tin, filling cups three-quarters full. Bake in preheated oven for 25 minutes.

HINT: To make 1 cup (250 mL) of sour milk, measure 1 tbsp (15 mL) vinegar or lemon juice into a measuring cup. Then fill to 1 cup (250 mL) with milk. Let stand about 5 minutes before using in your recipe.

Peanut Butter Muffins

2 cups	all-purpose flour	500 mL
1 tbsp	baking powder	15 mL
1/2 tsp	salt	2 mL
1 1/4 cups	milk	300 mL
1	egg	1
3 tbsp	granulated sugar	45 mL
1/2 cup	peanut butter	125 mL

Preheat oven to 400° F (200° C)
Muffin tin, paper-lined

1. In a large bowl, mix together flour, baking powder and salt. Make a well in the center.

2. In an electric blender, combine milk, egg, sugar and peanut butter. Cover and blend until thoroughly mixed. Add all at once to dry ingredients and stir just until moistened. Do not overmix.

3. Spoon batter into prepared muffin tin, filling cups three-quarters full. Bake in preheated oven for 25 to 30 minutes or until golden brown.

Peanut Butter Banana Muffins

2 cups	all-purpose flour	500 mL
1/2 cup	packed brown sugar	125 mL
1 tbsp	baking powder	15 mL
1/4 tsp	salt	1 mL
1/2 cup	peanut butter (chunky or smooth)	125 mL
2 tbsp	vegetable oil	25 mL
2	eggs	2
3/4 cup	milk	175 mL
2	medium bananas, mashed	2

Preheat oven to 400° F (200° C)
Muffin tin, greased or paper-lined

1. In a large bowl, combine flour, brown sugar, baking powder and salt.

2. In another bowl, combine peanut butter, oil, eggs, milk and mashed bananas. Add to flour mixture, stirring just until moistened and blended.

3. Spoon batter evenly into prepared muffin tin. Bake in preheated oven for 20 minutes or until done.

Crunchy Peanut Butter and Jelly Muffins

2 cups	all-purpose flour	500 mL
1/2 cup	granulated sugar	125 mL
2 1/2 tsp	baking powder	12 mL
1/2 tsp	salt	2 mL
3/4 cup	crunchy peanut butter	175 mL
3/4 cup	milk	175 mL
2	eggs	2
1/4 cup	jam or jelly	50 mL

Preheat oven to 400° F (200° C)
Muffin tin, paper-lined

1. In a large bowl, mix together flour, sugar, baking powder and salt. With a pastry blender or two knives, cut in peanut butter until mixture resembles coarse crumbs. Add milk and eggs all at once, stirring just until moistened and blended.

2. Spoon 2 tbsp (25 mL) batter into each prepared cup. Put 1 tsp (5 mL) jam or jelly in center of each. Top with another 2 tbsp (25 mL) batter. Bake in preheated oven for about 20 minutes.

HINT: Use muffin tins to make extra-large ice cubes for punch.

Peanut Butter Oat Muffins

1 1/2 cups	whole-wheat flour	375 mL
1 1/2 cups	rolled oats	375 mL
4 tsp	baking powder	20 mL
1 tsp	salt	5 mL
1 tsp	baking soda	5 mL
1/2 cup	raisins	125 mL
1 cup	plain yogurt	250 mL
3/4 cup	liquid honey	175 mL
1/2 cup	peanut butter	125 mL
1/3 cup	vegetable oil	75 mL
3	eggs, lightly beaten	3
1 tsp	vanilla	5 mL

Preheat oven to 375° F (190° C)
Muffin tin, greased or paper-lined

1. In a large bowl, combine flour, oats, baking powder, salt and baking soda. Stir in raisins.

2. In another bowl, beat together yogurt, honey, peanut butter, oil, eggs and vanilla until smooth. Add to dry ingredients and stir just until moistened and blended. Do not overmix.

3. Spoon batter into prepared muffin tin, filling cups three-quarters full. Bake in preheated oven for 25 to 30 minutes or until done.

HINT: For a special treat, spread peanut butter on butter cookies or vanilla wafers. Place a toasted marshmallow between two cookies or wafers and press together slightly and — *voila!* — a Peanut Butter Puff.

Here we use paper drink cups as a fun alternative to standard muffin cups.

Peanut Pops

1 cup	finely crushed peanut brittle	250 mL
4 cups	vanilla ice cream	1 L
8 tbsp	peanut butter	125 mL

8-cup muffin tin
Eight 5-oz (150 mL) paper drinking cups
Eight plastic spoons

1. Place a paper cup in each ungreased muffin tin cup. Add 1 tbsp (15 mL) peanut brittle to each. Spoon in some ice cream to half fill each cup. Add 1 tbsp (15 mL) peanut butter and then remaining ice cream. Top with remaining peanut brittle.

2. With the back of a spoon, pack mixture down firmly. Insert a plastic spoon, bowl-end down, into each cup. Wrap each cup in foil and place muffin tin in freezer.

3. When firm, peel off foil, lift out cups and eat ice cream on a stick. Or leave cups on, pull out spoon and enjoy an ice cream sundae.

Pepperoni Muffins

2 1/2 cups	all-purpose flour	625 mL
1/4 cup	grated Parmesan cheese	50 mL
2 tbsp	packed brown sugar	25 mL
1 tbsp	baking powder	15 mL
1/2 tsp	salt	2 mL
1 tsp	oregano or basil leaves	5 mL
1 cup	chopped pepperoni (casings removed)	250 mL
1	pkg (4 oz [125 g]) softened cream cheese	1
1 cup	milk	250 mL
2	eggs	2
1/2 cup	margarine or butter, melted	125 mL

Preheat oven to 400° F (200° C)
Muffin tin, greased or paper-lined

1. In a large bowl, combine flour, cheese, brown sugar, baking powder, salt, oregano and pepperoni.

2. In another bowl, beat softened cream cheese, gradually adding milk. Add eggs, one at a time, and beat well. Stir in margarine. Add to flour mixture, stirring just until moistened.

3. Spoon batter into prepared muffin tin, filling cups to the top. Bake in preheated oven for about 20 minutes. Serve warm.

Pizza Muffins

1 1/2 cups	chopped pepperoni sausage	375 mL
1	green pepper, seeded and finely chopped	1
1	can (10 oz [284 mL]) sliced mushrooms	1
1	medium onion, finely chopped	1
1 1/4 cups	grated cheese (such as Monterey Jack)	300 mL
1/2 cup	pizza sauce	125 mL
2 tsp	garlic powder	10 mL
5	eggs	5
1/4 cup	vegetable oil	50 mL
1 1/4 cups	all-purpose flour	300 mL
1 tbsp	baking powder	15 mL

Preheat oven to 375° F (190° C)
Muffin tin, greased

1. In a large bowl, combine pepperoni, green pepper, mushrooms, onion, cheese, pizza sauce and garlic powder.

2. In another bowl, beat eggs. Blend in oil, then flour and baking powder. Beat until smooth. Stir in pepperoni mixture and mix until well blended.

3. Spoon batter into prepared muffin tin. Bake in preheated oven for 20 to 25 minutes or until lightly browned.

Mini Pumpkin Muffins

1 3/4 cups	all-purpose flour	425 mL
1/2 cup	packed brown sugar	125 mL
1 tsp	baking powder	5 mL
1/2 tsp	baking soda	2 mL
1/2 tsp	salt	2 mL
1/2 tsp	cinnamon	2 mL
1/4 tsp	ground nutmeg	1 mL
3/4 cup	canned pumpkin	175 mL
1/2 cup	vegetable oil	125 mL
2/3 cup	milk	150 mL

Preheat oven to 350° F (180° C)
Miniature muffin tin, greased

1. In a large bowl, mix together flour, brown sugar, baking powder, baking soda, salt, cinnamon and nutmeg.

2. In another bowl, combine pumpkin, oil and milk until well-blended. Add to flour mixture and stir just until moistened and blended. Do not overmix.

3. Spoon batter into prepared miniature muffin tin, filling cups to the top. Bake in preheated oven for 12 to 15 minutes.

Puffed Wheat Morsels

1/4 cup	butter *or* margarine	50 mL
1/4 cup	packed brown sugar	50 mL
1/4 cup	corn syrup	50 mL
3 cups	sugar-coated puffed wheat cereal (or puffed rice or corn)	750 mL

Muffin tin, greased or paper-lined

1. In a heavy saucepan over medium heat, melt butter with sugar and corn syrup. Cook until bubbly and slightly thick. Be careful – it gets very hot. Remove from heat, holding onto handle tightly.

2. Pour in cereal and stir quickly with a wooden spoon. Drop by spoonfuls into prepared muffin tin. Allow to cool before serving.

Quick Mix Muffins

1 cup	buttermilk baking mix	250 mL
3 tbsp	granulated sugar	45 mL
1	egg	1
1/3 cup	water	75 mL

Preheat oven to 400° F (200° C)
6- or 8-cup muffin tin, paper-lined

1. In a large bowl, mix together baking mix, sugar and egg. Add water and beat vigorously with a mixing spoon for 1 minute.

2. Spoon batter evenly into prepared muffin tin. Bake in preheated oven for 15 to 20 minutes.

VARIATION

Add 1/4 cup (50 mL) chopped nuts to batter before spooning into muffin tins.

Spicy Spice Muffins

2 cups	all-purpose flour	500 mL
3 tsp	baking powder	15 mL
1 tsp	salt	5 mL
1 tsp	ground ginger	5 mL
1 tsp	ground nutmeg	5 mL
1 tsp	cinnamon	5 mL
1	egg, well-beaten	1
1/2 cup	granulated sugar	125 mL
1/4 cup	butter or margarine, melted	50 mL
1 cup	milk	250 mL

Preheat oven to 425° F (220° C)
Muffin tin, greased or paper-lined

1. In a large bowl, combine flour, baking powder, salt, ginger, nutmeg and cinnamon.

2. In another bowl, combine egg, sugar, melted butter and milk. Add to the flour mixture, stirring just until moistened and blended.

3. Spoon batter into prepared muffin tin, filling cups two-thirds to three-quarters full. Bake in preheated oven for 15 to 20 minutes or until toothpick inserted in the center of a muffin comes out clean and dry.

Buffins, Cuffins & Puffins

H ere's a new great way to please your family and friends. Buffins, Cuffins, Puffins — call them what you like — they are like a little bit of biscuit, a little bit of cupcake, a little bit of muffin, but a whole lot delicious for breakfasts, snacks, lunches or desserts.

All of these recipes can be baked in your regular cupcake or muffin pans. There are other fancier pans, or special little individual bundt pans that you can use.

Buffins

2 cups	milk	500 mL
1/2 cup	butter *or* margarine	125 mL
4 tbsp	granulated sugar	60 mL
1 tsp	salt	5 mL
1 tbsp	granular yeast	15 mL
1/4 cup	very warm water	50 mL
2	eggs, beaten	2
4 cups	all-purpose flour	1 L

Preheat oven to 400° F (200° C)
Muffin tin, greased

1. In a saucepan over medium heat, scald the milk. Add butter, sugar and salt. Set aside to cool.

2. Dissolve yeast in the very warm water. Add to scalded milk mixture. Add beaten eggs and flour, beating until smooth. Let rise for 1 1/2 hours.

3. Beat batter down and spoon into prepared muffin tin, filling cups no more than half full. Set aside and let rise again for 1/2 hour. Bake in preheated oven for 12 to 15 minutes. This recipe should yield 16 to 24 buffins.

Apple Doughnut Buffins

1 1/2 cups	all-purpose flour	375 mL
1/2 cup	granulated sugar	125 mL
1 3/4 tsp	baking powder	9 mL
1/2 tsp	salt	2 mL
1/2 tsp	ground nutmeg	2 mL
1/3 cup	shortening	75 mL
1	egg	1
1/4 cup	milk	50 mL
1/2 cup	grated apple	125 mL
TOPPING		
1/2 cup	butter, melted	125 mL
1/2 cup	granulated sugar	125 mL
1 1/2 tsp	cinnamon	7 mL

Preheat oven to 350° F (180° C)
Muffin tin, greased

1. In a large bowl, sift together flour, sugar, baking powder, salt and nutmeg. With a pastry blender, cut in shortening.

2. In another bowl, combine egg, milk and grated apple. Add to flour mixture.

3. Spoon batter into prepared muffin tin, filling cups two-thirds full. Bake in preheated oven for 20 to 25 minutes. Remove from pan.

4. In a bowl combine butter, sugar and cinnamon. Roll buffins in topping. Serve warm.

Baked 'Donut' Buffins

1/4 cup	butter *or* margarine	50 mL
6 tbsp	granulated sugar	90 mL
1	egg	1
1/2 tsp	vanilla	2 mL
1 1/4 cups	all-purpose flour	300 mL
2 tsp	baking powder	10 mL
Dash	salt	Dash
1/4 tsp	ground nutmeg	1 mL
1/3 cup	milk	75 mL
SUGAR-CINNAMON MIX		
1/2 cup	sugar	125 mL
1 to 1 1/2 tsp	cinnamon	5 to 7 mL

Preheat oven to 375° F (190° C)
Muffin tin, greased or paper-lined

1. In a large bowl, cream together butter and sugar. Add egg and vanilla, then flour, baking powder, salt, nutmeg and milk. Mix only until blended.

2. Spoon batter into prepared muffin tin. Bake in preheated oven for 15 minutes.

3. In a small bowl, mix together sugar and cinnamon until well blended. Remove muffins from tins and roll in topping.

Caraway Rye Buffins

2	pkgs active dry yeast	2
1/2 cup	warm water	125 mL
1/2 tsp	granulated sugar	2 mL
3 cups	all-purpose flour	750 mL
1 1/2 cups	rye flour	375 mL
2 tsp	salt	10 mL
1/4 tsp	baking soda	1 mL
2 tbsp	caraway seeds	25 mL
8 oz	low-fat plain yogurt	250 g
1/2 cup	butter or margarine, melted	125 mL
2	eggs	2
GLAZE		
1	egg white mixed with 1 tbsp (15 mL) water	1
TOPPING		
	Additional caraway seeds	

Preheat oven to 350° F (180° C)
Two 12-cup muffin tins, greased

1. In a large bowl, sprinkle yeast over warm water and sugar. Let stand for 5 minutes to allow yeast to soften.

2. In another bowl, combine all-purpose flour, rye flour, salt, baking soda and seeds.

3. In another bowl, whisk together yogurt, butter and eggs. Add to yeast mixture and mix until blended. Add half of flour mixture and beat on medium-high speed for 1 minute. Add remaining flour and continue beating until well blended. Cover with a towel and place in a warm spot away from drafts. Let rise for 1 hour or until doubled in size.

4. Punch down dough. Divide evenly into prepared muffin tins. Cover again and let rise in warm spot for 45 minutes or until doubled.

5. Brush tops with glaze. Sprinkle with caraway seeds. Bake in preheated oven for 20 to 25 minutes or until golden brown.

Citrus Upside-Down Buffins

2 cups	undrained canned grapefruit sections	500 mL
1	can (10 oz [284 mL]) mandarin orange sections, undrained	1
1/2 cup	packed brown sugar	125 mL
3 tbsp	all-purpose flour	45 mL
3 tbsp	butter or margarine	45 mL
1 cup	all-purpose flour	250 mL
1 tbsp	granulated sugar	15 mL
1 1/2 tsp	baking powder	7 mL
1/4 tsp	salt	1 mL
4 tbsp	butter or margarine	60 mL
	Milk	
1	egg, slightly beaten	1
	Granulated sugar	
	Cinnamon	

Preheat oven to 425° F (220° C)
Large ramekins

1. In a small bowl, mix together the undrained grapefruit and mandarin orange sections. Spoon evenly into ramekins.

2. In another small bowl, mix together brown sugar and 3 tbsp (45 mL) flour. Sprinkle over fruit and dot with 3 tbsp (45 mL) butter. Bake in preheated oven for 15 minutes.

3. In a large bowl, combine flour, sugar, baking powder and salt. Cut in 4 tbsp (50 mL) butter.

4. In a measuring cup, add enough milk to beaten egg to make 1/2 cup (125 mL). Add to flour mixture. Stir until well blended.

5. Drop batter by spoonfuls over hot fruit cups to form biscuits. Sprinkle with sugar and cinnamon. Bake in preheated oven for 20 to 25 minutes or until golden brown. Serve warm.

Praline Buffins

1/2 cup	butter	125 mL
1/2 cup	packed brown sugar	125 mL
	Cinnamon	
36	pecan or walnut halves	36
2 cups	biscuit baking mix	500 mL
1/3 cup	applesauce	75 mL
1/3 cup	milk	75 mL

Preheat oven to 450° F (230° C)
12-cup muffin tin

1. Put 2 tsp (10 mL) butter in each muffin cup. Heat in preheated oven until butter is melted. Stir 2 tsp (10 mL) brown sugar and a pinch of cinnamon into butter in each cup. Add 3 nut halves to each.

2. In a large bowl, combine biscuit mix, applesauce and milk. Mix well until a dough forms. Spoon batter into muffin cups. Bake in preheated oven for 10 minutes.

3. Invert whole pan immediately onto a plate and let sit for 5 minutes, allowing syrup to run down over buffins. Remove the pan and serve warm.

HINT: To get walnut meats out whole, soak nuts overnight in salt water before cracking.

The surprise in this buffin recipe is that the delicious fruit flavor comes from a can of instant drink mix.

It usually yields 36 to 40 buffins.

1/2 cup	strawberry-flavored drink mix	125 mL
3/4 cup	milk	175 mL
1	egg	1
2 tbsp	vegetable oil	25 mL
2 cups	biscuit mix	500 mL
	Icing sugar	

Miniature Strawberry Buffins

Preheat oven to 400° F (200° C)
Miniature muffin tin, greased

1. In a small bowl, combine drink mix, milk, egg and oil. Beat with a fork until well blended.

2. In a large bowl, combine biscuit mix and wet ingredients. Stir just until biscuit mix is completely moistened. The batter will be soft.

3. Spoon batter into prepared muffin tin, filling cups two-thirds full. Bake in preheated oven for 10 minutes or until delicately golden but not browned.

4. Remove buffins from pan and sprinkle tops with icing sugar. Serve hot.

Wheat Germ Cornmeal Buffins

2	eggs, slightly beaten	2
2 tbsp	milk	25 mL
1	pkg active dry yeast	1
1/4 cup	very warm water (not boiling)	50 mL
1/4 cup	granulated sugar	50 mL
1/4 cup	butter, melted	50 mL
1/2 tsp	salt	2 mL
1/4 cup	yellow cornmeal	50 mL
1/2 cup	dry currants or raisins	125 mL
1 cup	milk	250 mL
1/4 cup	wheat germ	50 mL
2 1/4 cups	all-purpose flour	550 mL

Preheat oven to 375° F (190° C)
Muffin tin, greased

1. In a small bowl, combine 2 tbsp (25 mL) of the beaten egg with 2 tbsp (25 mL) milk. Set aside.

2. In a large mixing bowl, dissolve yeast in warm water. Let stand for 5 minutes. Mix in the remaining egg, sugar, butter, salt, cornmeal and currants. Stir in milk and wheat germ, blending well. Add flour gradually and beat until smooth. Cover loosely with a towel or waxed paper and place in a warm spot. Let rise for 1 hour or until doubled in size.

3. Punch dough down or beat well. Spoon into prepared muffin tin. Cover again and let rise in a warm spot for 30 minutes or until muffin tin is full.

4. Lightly beat the reserved egg and milk and brush over tops. Sprinkle with additional wheat germ, if desired. Bake in preheated oven for 15 to 20 minutes or until browned.

HINT: When making any recipe requiring egg whites only, drop the yolks into a pan of boiling, salted water. Use these hard-cooked yolks for salads or sandwich fillings.

Cuffins

1/3 cup	softened shortening	75 mL
2 cups	sifted cake flour	500 mL
1 cup	granulated sugar	250 mL
2 1/2 tsp	baking powder	12 mL
3/4 tsp	salt	4 mL
3/4 cup	milk	175 mL
1	egg, slightly beaten	1
1 tsp	vanilla	5 mL

Preheat oven to 400° F (200° C)
Muffin tin, paper-lined

1. In a large bowl, cream shortening until well softened. Add cake flour, sugar, baking powder and salt, mixing until blended. Add half the milk and egg, mixing until flour is dampened. Add remaining milk and vanilla and stir just until moistened and well blended (or beat for 2 minutes with a hand mixer).

2. Spoon batter evenly into prepared muffin tin. Bake in preheated oven for 20 minutes or until done.

Apple Spice Cuffins

2	apples, pared, cored and diced	2
1/4 cup	water	50 mL
1 1/4 cups	all-purpose flour	300 mL
2 tbsp	unsweetened cocoa	25 mL
1/2 cup	granulated sugar	125 mL
1/2 tsp	baking powder	2 mL
1 tsp	baking soda	5 mL
1/2 tsp	salt	2 mL
1/2 tsp	cinnamon	2 mL
1/2 tsp	ground allspice	2 mL
2	egg yolks	2
1/4 cup	raisins	50 mL

Preheat oven to 350° F (180° C)
Two 8-cup muffin tins, paper-lined

1. In a small saucepan over medium heat, combine apples and water. Simmer, covered, for 5 minutes or until tender. Set aside to cool.

2. In a large bowl, combine flour, cocoa, sugar, baking powder, baking soda, salt, cinnamon and allspice. Add apples and egg yolks, beating until blended. Fold in raisins.

3. Spoon batter into prepared muffin tins, dividing evenly. Bake in preheated oven for about 30 minutes.

Banana Nut Cuffins

2 cups	all-purpose flour	500 mL
1 2/3 cups	granulated sugar	400 mL
1 1/4 tsp	baking powder	6 mL
1 1/4 tsp	baking soda	6 mL
1 tsp	salt	5 mL
2/3 cup	shortening	150 mL
2/3 cup	buttermilk	150 mL
3	eggs	3
1 1/4 cups	mashed bananas	300 mL
1/2 cup	chopped walnuts or pecans	125 mL
	Icing sugar	

Preheat oven to 350° F (180° C)
Two 12-cup muffin tins, paper-lined

1. In a large bowl, combine flour, sugar, baking powder, baking soda, salt, shortening, buttermilk, eggs, bananas and walnuts. Mix at low speed, scraping sides, then beat on high speed for 3 minutes.

2. Spoon batter into prepared muffin tins, filling cups three-quarters full. Bake in preheated oven for 20 to 25 minutes. When cuffins cool, dust with icing sugar.

HINT: To separate eggs use a small funnel, cracking egg open over the funnel. The white will run through while the yoke will remain in the funnel.

Black Bottom Cuffins

1 1/2 cups	all-purpose flour	375 mL
1/2 tsp	baking powder	2 mL
1/2 tsp	baking soda	2 mL
1/4 cup	unsweetened cocoa	50 mL
1 cup	granulated sugar	250 mL
1/2 tsp	salt	2 mL
1 cup	water	250 mL
1 tsp	vanilla	5 mL
6 tbsp	vegetable oil	90 mL
FILLING		
4 oz	softened cream cheese	125 g
1	egg, beaten	1
6 tbsp	granulated sugar	90 mL
1/2 cup	semi-sweet chocolate chips	125 mL

Preheat oven to 400° F (200° C)
Muffin tin, paper-lined

1. In a large bowl, mix together flour, baking powder, baking soda, cocoa, sugar and salt.

2. In another bowl, combine water, vanilla and oil. Pour into dry ingredients and stir well. Spoon batter into prepared muffin tin, about 2 tbsp (25 mL) each.

3. In another bowl, mix together cream cheese, egg, sugar and chocolate chips. Spoon 1 tbsp (15 mL) over batter and top with remaining batter. Bake in preheated oven for 20 minutes or until toothpick inserted in center comes out clean.

Brownie Chip Cuffins

3	squares semi-sweet baking chocolate	3
1/2 cup	butter	125 mL
2	eggs	2
1 1/2 cups	packed light brown sugar	375 mL
1 1/2 tsp	vanilla	7 mL
1 tbsp	strong black coffee	15 mL
1 tsp	cinnamon	5 mL
1	mashed ripe banana	1
1 cup	all-purpose flour	250 mL
1 cup	white chocolate chips (optional)	250 mL

Preheat oven to 350° F (180° C)
Muffin tin, paper-lined

1. In a small saucepan over low heat, melt chocolate with butter, stirring gently. Set aside to cool.

2. In a large bowl, whisk together eggs, sugar, vanilla, coffee and cinnamon. Add mashed banana and drizzle with chocolate, stirring lightly. Add flour, stirring just until moistened and blended. Fold in chocolate chips.

3. Spoon batter into prepared muffin tin, filling cups three-quarters full. Bake in preheated oven for 20 to 25 minutes or until a toothpick inserted in the center comes out dry and clean.

Cherry Cuffins

3	eggs	3
1/2 cup	shortening, melted	125 mL
3/4 cup	milk	175 mL
1 tsp	vanilla	5 mL
1 1/2 cups	all-purpose flour	375 mL
1 1/4 cups	granulated sugar	300 mL
2 tsp	baking powder	10 mL
Pinch	salt	Pinch
1 lb	cherries, pitted and chopped	500 g

Preheat oven to 400° F (200° C)
Muffin tin, paper-lined

1. In a bowl combine eggs, shortening, milk and vanilla. Mix well.

2. In a large bowl, combine flour, sugar, baking powder and salt. Add cherries and stir into egg mixture. Do not overmix.

3. Spoon batter into prepared muffin tin, filling cups two-thirds full. Bake in preheated oven for about 25 minutes.

LEMON CREAM CUFFIN TARTS (PAGE 68) ➤

Old-Fashioned Chocolate Cuffins

1/2 cup	shortening	125 mL
1 cup	granulated sugar	250 mL
2	eggs, separated and beaten	2
2 cups	all-purpose flour	500 mL
2 tsp	baking powder	10 mL
1/4 tsp	salt	1 mL
1/4 tsp	baking soda	1 mL
3/4 cup	milk	175 mL
1 tsp	vanilla	5 mL
2 1/2	squares unsweetened chocolate, melted	2 1/2

Preheat oven to 375° F (190° C)
Muffin tin, greased or paper-lined

1. In a large bowl, cream together shortening and sugar. Add beaten egg yolks.

2. In another bowl, combine flour, baking powder, salt and baking soda. Add to creamed mixture alternately with milk. Add vanilla and melted chocolate.

3. In another bowl, beat egg whites until stiff. Fold into mixture and blend well.

4. Spoon batter into prepared muffin tin, filling each cup to the top. Bake in preheated oven for 25 minutes or until done.

Chocolate Chip Cuffins

1/3 cup	softened shortening	75 mL
3/4 cup	granulated sugar	175 mL
2	eggs	2
1 tsp	vanilla	5 mL
2 1/4 cups	sifted cake flour	550 mL
3 tsp	double-acting baking powder	15 mL
1 tsp	salt	5 mL
2/3 cup	milk	150 mL
1	pkg (8 oz [250 g]) chocolate chips	1

Preheat oven to 375° F (190° C)
Muffin tin, paper-lined

1. In a large bowl, cream together shortening and sugar. With a spoon, mix in eggs one at a time. Add vanilla.

2. In another bowl, combine flour, baking powder and salt. Add to the shortening mixture alternately with milk.

3. Spoon batter into prepared muffin tin, filling cups half full. Sprinkle with half the chocolate chips. Top with remaining batter and sprinkle with remaining chocolate chips. Bake in preheated oven for 20 to 25 minutes.

≺ Deluxe Pizza Muffins (Page 109)

Chocolate Cream Cheese Cuffins

1	pkg (8 oz [250 g]) softened cream cheese	1
1	egg	1
1/3 cup	granulated sugar	75 mL
1 cup	chocolate chipits	250 mL
3 cups	all-purpose flour	750 mL
2 cups	granulated sugar	500 mL
1/2 cup	instant chocolate drink powder	125 mL
1 tsp	salt	5 mL
2 tsp	baking soda	10 mL
2 tsp	vanilla	10 mL
2 tbsp	vinegar	25 mL
2 cups	water	500 mL
2/3 cup	vegetable oil	150 mL

Preheat oven to 350° F (180° C)
Two 12-cup muffin tins, greased or paper-lined

1. In a small bowl, mix together cream cheese, egg and sugar. Add chipits and blend well. Set aside.

2. In a large bowl, combine flour, sugar, chocolate powder, salt and baking soda, mixing well. Add vanilla, vinegar, water and oil. Beat on low speed just until well blended.

3. Spoon batter into prepared muffin tins, filling cups two-thirds full. Drop 1 heaping tsp (5 mL) cheese mixture into each prepared muffin cup. Bake in preheated oven for 20 to 25 minutes.

VARIATIONS

🧁 For a quick version of this recipe, use 1 pkg chocolate cake mix (the 2 layer size). Mix according to package directions and bake as above.

🧁 You can use chocolate pieces or chunks in place of the chipits.

HINT: Make spice cuffins from a white or yellow cake mix by adding cinnamon, cloves and nutmeg.

Cocoa Raisin Cuffins

1 1/4 cups	all-purpose flour	300 mL
1 cup	granulated sugar	250 mL
3/4 tsp	baking soda	4 mL
1/2 tsp	cinnamon	2 mL
1/4 tsp	ground nutmeg	1 mL
1/4 tsp	salt	1 mL
1/4 cup	butter or margarine, melted (about 1 stick)	50 mL
1/4 cup	cocoa	50 mL
3/4 cup	applesauce	175 mL
1	egg, slightly beaten	1
1/2 cup	raisins	125 mL

Preheat oven to 350° F (180° C)
Muffin tin, greased or paper-lined

1. In a large bowl, mix together flour, sugar, baking soda, cinnamon, nutmeg and salt. Make a well in the center.

2. In another bowl, blend together butter and cocoa. Add applesauce and pour into flour mixture. Add egg, stirring just until moistened and blended. Fold in raisins.

3. Spoon batter into prepared muffin tin, filling cups three-quarters full. Bake in preheated oven for 20 minutes.

Coconut Chiffon Cuffins

2 1/4 cups	sifted cake-and-pastry flour	550 mL
1 1/2 cups	granulated sugar	375 mL
3 tsp	baking powder	15 mL
1 tsp	salt	5 mL
1/3 cup	vegetable oil	75 mL
1 cup	milk	250 mL
1 1/2 tsp	vanilla	7 mL
2	eggs, separated	2
1 cup	flaked coconut	250 mL

Preheat oven to 400° F (200° C)
Muffin tin, paper-lined

1. In a large mixer bowl, combine flour, 1 cup (250 mL) sugar, baking powder and salt. Make a well in the center. Add oil, half the milk and vanilla. Beat for 1 minute on medium speed. Add remaining milk and egg yolks. Beat again for 1 minute.

2. In a small mixer bowl, beat egg whites until soft peaks form. Gradually add remaining 1/2 cup (125 mL) sugar and beat until stiff peaks form. Fold into the batter.

3. Spoon batter into prepared muffin tin, filling cups three-quarters full. Top with coconut. Bake in preheated oven for about 15 minutes.

Fudgey Cuffins

2/3 cup	packed brown sugar	150 mL
1/3 cup	milk	75 mL
2	squares unsweetened chocolate	2
1/3 cup	softened shortening	75 mL
2/3 cup	packed brown sugar	150 mL
1 tsp	vanilla	5 mL
2	eggs	2
1 1/3 cups	all-purpose flour	325 mL
1 tsp	baking soda	5 mL
1/2 tsp	salt	2 mL
1/2 cup	milk	125 mL

Preheat oven to 375° F (190° C)
Muffin tin, paper-lined

1. In a saucepan over very low heat, combine 2/3 cup (150 mL) brown sugar, 1/3 cup (75 mL) milk and chocolate, stirring until chocolate melts. Set aside to cool.

2. In a large bowl, cream together shortening and 2/3 cup (150 mL) brown sugar until light and fluffy. Add vanilla and eggs, one at a time. Beat well after each addition.

3. In another bowl, combine flour, baking soda and salt. Add to creamed mixture alternately with 1/2 cup (125 mL) milk, beating after each addition. Add chocolate mixture.

4. Spoon batter into prepared muffin tin, filling cups three-quarters full. Bake in preheated oven for about 20 minutes.

Lemon Cream Cuffin Tarts

1	roll refrigerated sugar cookie dough	1
1	pkg lemon pudding and pie filling	1
1 tsp	grated lemon zest	5 mL
	Sweetened whipped cream	
	Strawberries, washed and hulled	

Preheat oven to 375° F (190° C)
Muffin tin, foil-lined

1. Unroll cookie dough and cut into 36 slices. Press into bottoms and up sides of prepared muffin tins. Bake in preheated oven for 10 minutes or until golden brown. Cool completely and then carefully peel off the foil. Set aside.

2. In a bowl, prepare pudding mix according to package directions. Stir in lemon zest and place in refrigerator.

3. When filling is chilled, spoon 1 tbsp (15 mL) into each cup. Return to refrigerator.

4. To serve, spoon some whipped cream on top. Place a whole strawberry, hull-side down, on top.

Lemon Streusel Cuffins

2 1/4 cups	sifted cake-and-pastry flour	550 mL
2 tsp	baking powder	10 mL
1/2 tsp	salt	2 mL
1 3/4 cups	granulated sugar	425 mL
1 tbsp	fresh lemon juice	15 mL
1 tsp	grated lemon zest	5 mL
8 oz	non-fat plain yogurt	250 g
3 tbsp	vegetable oil	45 mL
1/2 tsp	vanilla	2 mL
4	large egg whites	4
STREUSEL TOPPING		
1/4 cup	firmly packed brown sugar	50 mL
1/4 cup	uncooked oats	50 mL
1/4 tsp	cinnamon	1 mL

Preheat oven to 350° F (180° C)
Two 12-cup muffin tins, paper-lined

1. In a large mixer bowl, combine flour, baking powder and salt.

2. In another bowl, beat together sugar, juice, zest, yogurt, oil and vanilla. Pour into flour mixture and beat on low speed just until well blended.

3. In a small bowl, beat egg whites until stiff peaks form. Fold into batter.

4. In another bowl, combine brown sugar, oats and cinnamon.

5. Spoon batter into prepared muffin tins, filling cups three-quarters full. Sprinkle with streusel topping. Bake in preheated oven for 35 to 40 minutes.

NOTE: I usually make the streusel topping first by mixing all the ingredients together in a bowl and then set it aside until needed.

HINT: When you buy cello-wrapped cupcakes or muffins and the wrapper is stuck to the frosting, hold the package under cold water for 1 minute. The wrapper will come off clean.

Lemon Sugar-Topped Cuffins

TOPPING

1 tbsp	granulated sugar	15 mL
1/2 tsp	grated lemon zest	2 mL

1 cup	self-rising flour	250 mL
1/2 cup	granulated sugar	125 mL
1/2 cup	milk	125 mL
1/3 cup	salad oil	75 mL
1 tsp	grated lemon zest	5 mL
1	egg	1
1/2 tsp	vanilla	2 mL

Preheat oven to 425° F (220° C)
Muffin tin, paper-lined

1. In a small bowl, combine sugar and grated lemon zest. Set aside.

2. In a large bowl, combine flour and sugar. Make a well in the center. Add milk, oil, lemon zest, egg and vanilla. Mix together until just moistened.

3. Spoon batter into prepared muffin tin. Sprinkle with topping. Bake in preheated oven for 15 minutes.

VARIATIONS

Jam Cuffins: Omit lemon zest and topping. Spoon batter into muffin tins and top each with 1 tsp (5 mL) seedless red raspberry jam. Swirl a thin knife or toothpick through batter and bake as above.

Mocha Chip Cuffins: Omit lemon zest and topping. Reduce milk to 1/4 cup (50 mL). Dissolve 2 tsp (10 mL) instant coffee in 1/4 cup (50 mL) hot water and combine with the milk. Fold in 1/3 cup (75 mL) mini chocolate chips and bake as above.

Sour Cream 'n' Spice Cuffins: Omit lemon zest and topping. Add 1/2 tsp (2 mL) cinnamon, pinch of cloves and nutmeg to the dry ingredients. Decrease the milk to 1/4 cup (50 mL) and combine with 1/4 cup (50 mL) sour cream. Make a topping of 1/2 cup (125 mL) chopped walnuts, 1 tbsp (15 mL) sugar and 1/4 tsp (1 mL) cinnamon. Sprinkle on top of each cuffin and bake as above.

Peanut Butter Cuffins

2 cups	all-purpose flour	500 mL
2 tsp	baking powder	10 mL
1/2 tsp	salt	2 mL
1/2 cup	peanut butter	125 mL
1/3 cup	softened shortening	75 mL
1 tsp	vanilla	5 mL
1 1/2 cups	packed brown sugar	375 mL
2	eggs	2
3/4 cup	milk	175 mL

Preheat oven to 375° F (190° C)
Muffin tin, paper-lined

1. In a large bowl, mix together flour, baking powder and salt.

2. In another bowl, cream together peanut butter, shortening and vanilla. Gradually add brown sugar, beating with a spoon until light and fluffy. Add eggs, one at a time, beating well after each addition. Add to flour mixture alternately with milk.

3. Spoon batter into prepared muffin tin, filling cups three-quarters full. Bake in preheated oven for 20 minutes.

NOTE: You can frost the cuffins with peanut butter and sprinkle with icing sugar.

Peanut Butter Chocolate Cuffins

2 cups	all-purpose flour	500 mL
2 cups	granulated sugar	500 mL
3/4 cup	dry cocoa	175 mL
1 tsp	baking soda	5 mL
1 tsp	salt	5 mL
1/2 tsp	baking powder	2 mL
3/4 cup	shortening	175 mL
3/4 cup	buttermilk	175 mL
3/4 cup	water	175 mL
2	eggs	2
1 tsp	vanilla	5 mL

PEANUT BUTTER CREAM ICING

6 oz	softened cream cheese	175 g
2/3 cup	creamy peanut butter	150 mL
1/4 cup	milk	50 mL
1 tsp	vanilla	5 mL
3 cups	icing sugar	750 mL

Preheat oven to 350° F (180° C)
Muffin tin, paper-lined

1. In a large mixer bowl, combine flour, sugar, cocoa, baking soda, salt and baking powder. Make a well in the center. Add shortening, buttermilk, water, eggs and vanilla. Beat on low speed for 30 seconds, scraping sides of bowl. Then beat on high speed for 3 minutes.

2. Spoon batter into prepared muffin tin, filling cups three-quarters full. Bake in preheated oven for 20 minutes or until toothpick inserted in center comes out dry. Remove from pan and cool completely.

3. Meanwhile, in a large bowl, beat together cream cheese and peanut butter. Add milk and vanilla, beating well. Gradually add icing sugar and beat until smooth. (If necessary, add additional milk until a smooth consistency is reached.) Spread over cooled cuffins.

NOTE: To make this cuffin even more special, take a pastry bag with a large star tip and fill with icing. Insert the tip into the center of each cuffin. Pipe some icing into the cuffin and add a swirl on top.

Pumpkin Nut Cuffins

2 1/4 cups	all-purpose flour	550 mL
3 tsp	baking powder	15 mL
1/2 tsp	baking soda	2 mL
1/2 tsp	salt	2 mL
3/4 tsp	ground ginger	4 mL
1/2 tsp	cinnamon	2 mL
1/2 tsp	ground nutmeg	2 mL
1/2 cup	softened butter or margarine	125 mL
1 1/3 cups	granulated sugar	325 mL
2	eggs, well beaten	2
1 cup	canned pumpkin purée *or* cooked pumpkin, mashed	250 mL
3/4 cup	milk	175 mL
3/4 cup	chopped pecans or walnuts	175 mL

Preheat oven to 375° F (190° C)
Muffin tin, greased or paper-lined

1. In a large bowl, combine flour, baking powder, baking soda, salt, ginger, cinnamon and nutmeg.

2. In another bowl, cream together butter and sugar until light and fluffy. Stir in eggs and pumpkin. Pour into dry ingredients alternately with milk, blending until smooth. Fold in the nuts.

3. Spoon batter into prepared muffin tin, filling cups three-quarters full. Bake in preheated oven for 25 minutes or until a toothpick inserted in center comes out clean.

NOTE: These cuffins are not very sweet, so if you have a sweet tooth, top them with your favorite frosting.

HINT: If you are using fresh pumpkin in a recipe, a 5 lb (2.5 kg) pumpkin yields about 4 1/2 cups (1.125 L) mashed pumpkin.

Sweet Chocolate Cuffins

2 cups	sifted cake-and-pastry flour	500 mL
2 tsp	baking powder	10 mL
1/2 tsp	salt	2 mL
1/4 cup	butter (about half a stick)	50 mL
3	squares unsweetened chocolate	3
2	eggs, separated	2
1 1/2 cups	granulated sugar	375 mL
1 1/3 cups	milk	325 mL
2 1/2 tsp	vanilla	12 mL
	Icing sugar	

Preheat oven to 375° F (190° C)
Muffin tin, paper-lined

1. In a large bowl, mix together flour, baking powder and salt.

2. In top of a double boiler over hot (not boiling) water, melt butter and chocolate.

3. In a small bowl, beat together egg yolks and sugar until well blended and lemon colored. Add chocolate mixture and blend well. Pour into flour mixture alternately with milk and vanilla. Beat on low speed until blended.

4. In another small bowl, beat egg whites until stiff peaks form. Fold gently into the batter.

5. Spoon batter into prepared muffin tin, filling cups to the top. Bake in preheated oven for about 20 minutes. Remove from pan and set aside to cool. Dust tops with icing sugar.

Applesauce Puffins

2 cups	packaged biscuit mix	500 mL
1/4 cup	granulated sugar	50 mL
1 tsp	cinnamon	5 mL
1/2 cup	applesauce	125 mL
1/4 cup	milk	50 mL
1	egg, beaten	1
2 tbsp	vegetable oil	25 mL
TOPPING		
2 tbsp	butter or margarine, melted	25 mL
1/4 cup	granulated sugar	50 mL
1/4 tsp	cinnamon	1 mL

Preheat oven to 400° F (200° C)
Muffin tin, greased or paper-lined

1. In a large bowl, mix together biscuit mix, sugar and cinnamon. Add applesauce, milk, egg and oil. Beat with a spoon for about 1 minute.

2. Spoon batter into prepared muffin tin, filling cups two-thirds full. Bake in preheated oven for 12 minutes or until golden brown. Cool slightly before removing from tins.

3. Dip slightly cooled puffins into melted butter, then into sugar and cinnamon.

NOTE: Try making these in a mini or petite muffin pan.

Apple Streusel Puffins

1/4 cup	butter, melted	50 mL
1/2 cup	granulated sugar	125 mL
1	egg, slightly beaten	1
1/2 cup	milk	125 mL
1 1/2 cups	all-purpose flour	375 mL
1 tbsp	baking powder	15 mL
1/2 tsp	salt	2 mL
1/2 tsp	cinnamon	2 mL
1 cup	grated apple	250 mL
TOPPING		
1/4 cup	granulated sugar	50 mL
1/2 tsp	cinnamon	2 mL
1/4 cup	chopped walnuts	50 mL

Preheat oven to 375° F (190° C)
Muffin tin, greased or paper-lined

1. In a large bowl, cream together butter and sugar. Stir in egg and milk. Add flour, baking powder, salt and cinnamon. Fold in apple.

2. Spoon batter into prepared muffin tin, filling cups two-thirds full.

3. In a bowl combine sugar, cinnamon and walnuts and sprinkle over puffins. Bake in preheated oven for about 20 minutes.

Cheese Puffin Popovers

1 cup	all-purpose flour	250 mL
1/2 tsp	salt	2 mL
2	eggs	2
1 cup	milk	250 mL
1/2 cup	grated Cheddar cheese	125 mL

Preheat oven to 425° F (220° C)
Six ramekins, greased
Cookie sheet

1. In a bowl combine flour and salt. Add eggs, milk and cheese, stirring until just smooth.

2. Spoon batter into ramekins, filling only half full. Set cups on cookie sheet.

3. Bake in preheated oven for 45 minutes or until golden brown. Do not open oven before done or the puffins will fall. Serve hot.

Chocolate Peanut Puffins

2 cups	biscuit mix	500 mL
2 tbsp	granulated sugar	25 mL
1/2 cup	creamy peanut butter	125 mL
3/4 cup	chocolate-covered peanuts	175 mL
1	egg	1
3/4 cup	milk	175 mL
2 tbsp	vegetable oil	25 mL

Preheat oven to 400° F (200° C)
Muffin tin, paper-lined

1. In a large bowl, combine biscuit mix and sugar. Cut in peanut butter until mixture is crumbly. Add peanuts, mixing well.

2. In a small bowl, beat egg slightly. Add milk and oil. Pour into peanut mixture and stir just until moistened.

3. Spoon batter into prepared muffin tin, filling cups three-quarters full. Bake in preheated oven for 20 minutes or until golden brown. Serve hot.

Double Chocolate Puffins

3	squares unsweetened chocolate	3
3/4 cup	milk	175 mL
6 tbsp	softened butter or margarine	90 mL
3/4 cup	granulated sugar	175 mL
2	eggs	2
1 tsp	vanilla	5 mL
3/4 cup	all-purpose flour	175 mL
1 1/2 tsp	baking powder	7 mL

Preheat oven to 350° F (180° C)
Ramekins or muffin tin, greased

1. In a saucepan over low heat, combine chocolate and milk until smooth. Set aside to cool.

2. In a large bowl, cream together butter and sugar. Add eggs, one at a time, mixing well. Add vanilla and stir in flour and baking powder. Stir in chocolate mixture.

3. Spoon batter into prepared ramekins. Bake in preheated oven for 20 to 25 minutes. Remove from oven and invert cups over a plate so that puffins are upside-down.

NOTE: For an added treat, whip 1/2 cup (125 mL) whipping cream and gradually stir in 1/2 cup (125 mL) slightly softened chocolate ice cream. Spoon over the inverted puffins.

Cinnamon Puffs

1 cup	all-purpose flour	250 mL
1/2 tsp	salt	2 mL
1 tsp	cinnamon	5 mL
3	eggs	3
1 cup	milk	250 mL
3 tbsp	butter or margarine, melted	45 mL

Preheat oven to 425° F (220° C)
Muffin tin, greased

1. In a blender combine flour, salt, cinnamon, eggs, milk and melted butter. Blend just until smooth.

2. Spoon batter into prepared muffin tin, filling cups three-quarters full. Bake in preheated oven for 15 to 20 minutes.

French Breakfast Puffins

1/3 cup	softened shortening	75 mL
1/2 cup	granulated sugar	125 mL
1	egg	1
1 1/2 cups	all-purpose flour *or* cake-and-pastry flour	375 mL
1 1/2 tsp	baking powder	7 mL
1/2 tsp	salt	2 mL
1/4 tsp	ground nutmeg	1 mL
1/2 cup	milk	125 mL
TOPPING		
1/2 cup	granulated sugar	125 mL
1 tsp	cinnamon	5 mL
1/2 cup	butter or margarine, melted	125 mL

Preheat oven to 350° F (180° C)
Muffin tin, greased

1. In a large bowl, cream shortening with 1/2 cup (125 mL) sugar and egg, blending well. Stir in flour, baking powder, salt and nutmeg alternately with milk.

2. Spoon batter into prepared muffin tin, filling cups two-thirds full. Bake in preheated oven for 20 to 25 minutes.

3. In a bowl combine 1/2 cup (125 mL) sugar and cinnamon. As soon as puffins are ready, remove from pan. Roll in melted butter, then into the sugar-cinnamon mixture. Serve immediately.

Ginger Lemon Puffins

4 tbsp	softened butter	60 mL
1/2 cup	granulated sugar	125 mL
1	egg	1
1 tsp	grated lemon zest	5 mL
2 cups	all-purpose flour	500 mL
4 tsp	baking powder	20 mL
1/2 tsp	salt	2 mL
1/4 tsp	ground nutmeg	1 mL
1 cup	milk	250 mL
3/4 cup	granulated sugar	175 mL
2 tsp	ground ginger	10 mL
1/2 cup	melted butter	125 mL

Preheat oven to 375° F (190° C)
Muffin tin, greased

1. In a bowl cream together butter and 1/2 cup (125 mL) sugar. Beat in egg and lemon zest.

2. In a large bowl, combine flour, baking powder, salt and nutmeg. Add creamed mixture alternately with milk, beating after each addition.

3. Spoon batter into prepared muffin tin, filling cups three-quarters full. Bake in preheated oven for 15 to 20 minutes.

4. Meanwhile, in a bowl combine 3/4 cup (175 mL) sugar and ginger. When puffins come out of the oven, immediately dip in melted butter, then in sugar-ginger mixture. Serve while warm.

Herbed Puffin Popovers

1 cup	all-purpose flour	250 mL
1/2 tsp	dried thyme	2 mL
1/4 tsp	nutmeg	1 mL
1/4 tsp	salt	1 mL
1 cup	milk	250 mL
1/2 tsp	Dijon mustard	2 mL
2 tbsp	vegetable oil	25 mL
2	eggs	2

Muffin tin, greased or paper-lined

1. In a large bowl, combine flour, thyme, nutmeg and salt. Make a well in the center.

2. In another bowl, whisk together milk, mustard, oil and eggs. Pour into flour mixture, whisking until smooth and blended.

3. Spoon batter into prepared muffin tin, filling cups three-quarters full. Bake at 450° F (230° C) for 15 minutes. Reduce heat to 375° F (190° C) and bake for 20 to 25 minutes or until crusty and golden brown.

NOTE: For this particular recipe it is best not to preheat the oven but to turn it on as you are placing the muffin tins inside.

Lemon Nutmeg Puffins

1 cup	whole-wheat bread flour	250 mL
1/2 tsp	grated nutmeg	2 mL
1/4 tsp	salt	1 mL
3	eggs	3
1 cup	milk	250 mL
1 tbsp	vegetable oil	15 mL
	Grated zest of 1 lemon	
2 tsp	butter *or* margarine	10 mL

Preheat oven to 450° F (230° C)
6-cup muffin tin, greased

1. In a bowl combine flour, nutmeg and salt.

2. In a blender process eggs. Gradually add flour mixture alternately with milk. Add oil and zest, blending until smooth. The batter should be thick.

3. Heat prepared muffin tins in preheated oven for a few minutes. Cut butter into 6 pieces and place a piece in each muffin cup. Return to oven until sizzling.

4. Spoon batter into muffin tin, filling cups two-thirds full. Bake in oven for 25 minutes.

NOTE: If you are not serving these immediately, puncture tops with a sharp knife to release the steam inside. Return pan to the turned-off oven, leaving door partially open, until you are ready to serve.

Orange Bran Puffins

1 cup	all-purpose flour	250 mL
1/2 tsp	baking powder	2 mL
3/4 tsp	baking soda	4 mL
1 tsp	salt	5 mL
3 tbsp	granulated sugar	45 mL
1 cup	bran	250 mL
1 tsp	grated orange zest	5 mL
1	egg	1
1 cup	buttermilk	250 mL
1 tbsp	butter or margarine, melted	15 mL

Preheat oven to 400° F (200° C)
Muffin tin, greased

1. In a large bowl, combine flour, baking powder, baking soda, salt and sugar. Stir in bran and grated orange zest.

2. In another bowl, beat egg slightly with buttermilk and melted butter. Add all at once to the flour mixture and stir just until moistened. Do not overmix. The batter will be lumpy.

3. Spoon batter into prepared muffin tin, filling cups three-quarters full. Bake in preheated oven for 15 minutes or until golden brown. Best served warm.

HINT: When making iced tea, add a little hot water and then cold water so that the crystals will dissolve more completely.

Parmesan Cheese Puffins

4	eggs	4
1 cup	milk	250 mL
2/3 cup	all-purpose flour	150 mL
1/2 cup	grated Parmesan cheese	125 mL
1/2 tsp	salt	2 mL

Preheat oven to 425° F (220° C)
Muffin tin or ramekins, greased

1. In a large mixer bowl, beat together eggs and milk. Add flour, cheese and salt, beating until well blended.

2. Spoon batter into prepared muffin tin, filling cups two-thirds full. Bake in preheated oven for 35 to 40 minutes.

Peanut Orange Breakfast Puffins

2 cups	all-purpose flour	500 mL
1 tbsp	baking powder	15 mL
1 tsp	salt	5 mL
1/4 cup	granulated sugar	50 mL
1	egg, beaten	1
1 cup	milk	250 mL
1/4 cup	peanut oil	50 mL
1/2 cup	chopped salted peanuts	125 mL
TOPPING		
1/4 cup	granulated sugar	50 mL
1 tsp	grated orange zest	5 mL
1/4 cup	butter or margarine, melted	50 mL

Preheat oven to 425° F (220° C)
Muffin tin or ramekins, greased

1. In a large bowl, combine flour, baking powder, salt and sugar.

2. In another bowl, combine egg, milk and peanut oil. Pour into flour mixture and stir just until moistened. Fold in peanuts.

3. Spoon batter into prepared muffin tin, filling cups two-thirds full. Bake in preheated oven for 15 to 20 minutes or until lightly brown.

4. In a bowl combine sugar and zest until crumbly. Dip puffin tops, hot from the oven, into melted butter and then into sugar mixture. Serve warm.

Pecan Lemon Honey Puffins

1 cup	all-purpose flour	250 mL
1/2 tsp	salt	2 mL
2	eggs	2
1 cup	milk (room temperature)	250 mL
3 tbsp	finely chopped pecans	45 mL
LEMON HONEY BUTTER		
6 tbsp	softened butter	90 mL
6 tbsp	honey	90 mL
	Finely grated zest of 1 lemon	

Preheat oven to 425° F (220° C)
6-cup muffin tin or six ramekins, greased

1. In a large bowl, combine flour and salt. Make a well in the center.

2. In another bowl, beat together eggs and milk. Pour into flour mixture, beating just until smooth. Fold in pecans.

3. Spoon batter into prepared muffin tin, filling cups two-thirds full. (If using custard cups, place them on a cookie sheet.) Bake in preheated oven for 25 to 30 minutes or until they puff up and are well browned.

4. In a bowl combine butter, honey and zest. Spread over warm puffins. Serve.

NOTE: Try other flavored spreads with these puffins.

Poppin' Puffins

2	eggs	2
1 cup	milk	250 mL
1 cup	all-purpose flour	250 mL
1/2 tsp	salt	2 mL
1 tbsp	vegetable oil	15 mL

Preheat oven to 450° F (230° C)
Six to eight ramekins, greased
Cookie sheet

1. In a large bowl, blend together eggs and milk. Beat in flour and salt. Add oil and beat another 1/2 minute. Do not overmix.

2. Spoon batter into prepared ramekins, filling cups only half full. Place cups on a cookie sheet. Bake in preheated oven for 10 minutes or until puffins pop. Then reduce heat to 350° F (180° C) and bake for 25 to 30 minutes or until firm and browned.

3. A few minutes before removing from oven, prick each puffin with a fork, allowing steam to escape. If you want puffins dry inside, turn off oven, keep door ajar and leave cups in for 30 minutes.

VARIATIONS

☕ **Cheese Puffins:** Mix 1/2 cup (125 mL) grated cheese into batter before filling cups.

☕ **Stuffed Puffins:** Split the puffins in half and fill with creamed vegetables, scrambled eggs or anything you like.

☕ **Whole-Wheat Puffins:** Replace half the all-purpose flour with whole-wheat flour.

Potato Cheese Puffins

1 1/4 cups	all-purpose flour	300 mL
1/4 cup	granulated sugar	50 mL
3 tsp	baking powder	15 mL
1 tsp	salt	5 mL
1 cup	instant potato flakes	250 mL
1	egg	1
1 cup	milk	250 mL
1/4 cup	vegetable oil	50 mL
1/2 cup	grated Cheddar cheese	125 mL

Preheat oven to 400° F (200° C)
Muffin tin or ramekins, greased

1. In a large bowl, mix together flour, sugar, baking powder, salt and 3/4 cup (175 mL) potato flakes.

2. In a smaller bowl, combine egg, milk and oil. Beat slightly until well blended. Pour into flour mixture and stir just until moistened and blended.

3. Spoon batter into prepared tin, filling cups two-thirds full. Sprinkle tops with grated cheese and remaining potato flakes. Bake in preheated oven for 15 to 20 minutes or until browned.

HINT: Keep oils in a squeeze bottle for when you need only a small amount of oil.

Red Cherry Puffins

2 1/2 cups	chopped canned red cherries (reserve 1/2 cup [125 mL] juice)	625 mL
1/2 cup	granulated sugar	125 mL
2 tbsp	quick-cooking tapioca	25 mL
2	egg whites	2
Dash	salt	Dash
1/4 tsp	cream of tartar	1 mL
2	egg yolks	2
1/3 cup	granulated sugar	75 mL
1/3 cup	sifted cake-and-pastry flour	75 mL

Preheat oven to 350° F (180° C)
Muffin tin, paper-lined

1. In a saucepan over medium heat, combine cherries, cherry juice, sugar and tapioca. Simmer for 5 minutes, stirring constantly. Set aside.

2. In a small bowl, beat egg whites until foamy. Add salt and cream of tartar. Beat until stiff peaks form.

3. In another bowl, beat egg yolks until thick and lemon-colored. Gradually add sugar, beating well. Fold into egg whites. Stir in flour.

4. Spoon cherry mixture into prepared muffin tin and pour batter over top. Bake in preheated oven for 25 to 30 minutes.

NOTE: Delicious served warm with ice cream.

Baked Salmon Puffins

3	eggs, separated	3
1	can (16 oz [455 mL]) salmon	1
3/4 cup	bread crumbs	175 mL
1 tbsp	finely chopped onion	15 mL
1 tbsp	lemon juice	15 mL
1/2 tsp	salt	2 mL
Dash	black pepper	Dash

Preheat oven to 300° F (150° C)
Four to six ramekins, greased
Baking pan

1. In a small bowl, beat egg whites until stiff peaks form. Set aside.

2. Drain salmon and remove any skin or small bones. Flake with a fork.

3. In a large bowl, beat egg yolks slightly. Add salmon, bread crumbs, onion, lemon juice, salt and pepper, mixing well. Fold in beaten egg whites.

4. Spoon batter into prepared ramekins. Place in baking pan with 1 inch (2.5 cm) boiling water. Bake in preheated oven for 45 to 50 minutes or until a knife inserted in the center of a puffin comes out clean.

NOTE: There are all kinds of prepared dips available in supermarkets that would be great with these puffins, especially one with sour cream, dill, onion, etc.

Here's a special treat and a break from using your muffin tins or custard cups. You use a cookie or baking sheet instead, but the end results are just as delicious.

2 cups	miniature marshmallows	500 mL
1/4 cup	granulated sugar	50 mL
1 cup	sour cream	250 mL
1 cup	water	250 mL
1/2 cup	butter *or* margarine	125 mL
1 cup	all-purpose flour	250 mL
1/4 tsp	salt	1 mL
4	eggs	4
4 cups	fresh strawberries, washed and hulled	1 L

Strawberry Drop Puffins

Baking sheet, greased

1. In a bowl combine marshmallows, sugar and sour cream. Cover and chill for several hours.

2. In a large saucepan over medium-high heat, bring water to a boil. Add butter, stirring until melted. Add flour and salt, stirring vigorously until mixture forms a ball. Remove from heat and cool slightly. Add eggs one at a time, beating after each addition.

3. Drop batter by heaping tablespoons (15 mL), about 3 inches apart on prepared baking sheet. Bake at 450° F (230° C) for 15 minutes. Reduce heat to 325° F (160° C) and bake for 25 minutes. Set aside to cool. Split puffins in half and remove any webbing inside.

4. In a bowl crush 2 cups (500 mL) strawberries. Slice the remaining 2 cups (500 mL). Fold all berries into chilled sour cream mixture. Spoon 1/4 cup (50 mL) filling into bottom half of each split puffin. Cover puffins with tops and spread with 1 tbsp (15 mL) filling.

NOTE: These are like an elegant, dressed-up version of a cream puff!

VARIATION

Strawberry Sundae Puffins: Fill split puffin halves with whipped cream and sliced fresh strawberries. Drizzle with a prepared fudge sauce and cover with the puffin tops. Dust lightly with icing sugar.

HINT: To keep strawberries fresh and firm, wash and remove caps (hull) just before using, not when storing, or they will absorb too much water and become mushy. Washing removes the natural protective covering. The hull protects the berry and helps preserve flavor, texture and nutrients.

Tuna Mushroom Puffins

4	eggs, slightly beaten	4
2 cups	soft bread crumbs	500 mL
1 tsp	salt	5 mL
1 tbsp	prepared mustard	15 mL
1 tbsp	minced onion	15 mL
2 cups	milk	500 mL
1	can (6 oz [170 g]) chunky-style tuna	1

SAUCE

1	can (10 oz [284 mL]) cream of mushroom soup	1
2 tbsp	butter	25 mL

Preheat oven to 400° F (200° C)
Ramekins, greased

1. In a large bowl, combine eggs, bread crumbs, salt, mustard, onion, milk and tuna. Pour evenly into prepared custard cups. Place cups in a large pan of hot water. Bake in preheated oven for 35 to 40 minutes.

2. In a saucepan over medium heat, combine cream of mushroom soup and butter. Spoon over puffins and serve warm.

Mix-A-Mix

Homemade Ready Mixes — It is quick and easy to make your own mixes to which all kinds of ingredients can be added. Most can be stored well in airtight containers in a cool, dry place. In this chapter, I will be providing you with recipes for basic mixes and also recipes using various mixes.

All 'Round Muffin Mix

7 cups	all-purpose flour	1.75 L
1 1/3 cups	non-fat dry milk	325 mL
3/4 cup	granulated sugar	175 mL
1/4 cup	double-acting baking powder	50 mL
1 tbsp	salt	15 mL

1. In a large bowl with a fork, combine flour, milk, sugar, baking powder and salt. Store in an airtight container in a cool, dry place.

Plain Muffins

2 cups	ALL 'ROUND MUFFIN MIX (see recipe above)	500 mL
1	egg, slightly beaten	1
1 cup	water	250 mL
3 tbsp	butter or margarine, melted	45 mL

Preheat oven to 400° F (200° C)
12-cup muffin tin, greased

1. Put muffin mix in a large bowl. In another bowl,, combine egg, water and melted butter. Add all at once to muffin mixture and stir just until moistened.

2. Spoon batter into prepared muffin tin, filling cups two-thirds full. Bake in preheated oven for 20 to 25 minutes.

VARIATIONS
☕ **Cheese Muffins:** Add a small piece of Cheddar cheese in the center of each muffin before baking.

☕ **Jelly Muffins:** Fill cups only half full with batter. Put 1 tsp (5 mL) of your favorite jelly in center of each muffin and top with remaining batter. Bake as directed.

Biscuit Mix No. 1

12 cups	all-purpose flour	3 L
4 tsp	cream of tartar	20 mL
4 tsp	baking soda	20 mL
4 tbsp	baking powder	60 mL
4 tbsp	granulated sugar	60 mL
1 2/3 cups	powdered milk	400 mL
1 lb	lard *or* shortening	500 g
3 tsp	salt	15 mL

1. In a bowl combine flour, cream of tartar, baking soda, baking powder, sugar, powdered milk, lard and salt.

2. Store mix in an airtight container in a cool, dry place. Use as you would any commercial mix.

Biscuit Mix No. 2

9 cups	all-purpose flour	2.25 L
1 tbsp	salt	15 mL
4 tbsp	baking powder	50 mL
2 cups	shortening (1 lb [500 g])	500 mL

1. In a large bowl, mix together flour, salt and baking powder. Add shortening, working in with a pastry blender (or fingers) until texture resembles coarse crumbs.

2. Store mix in an airtight container in a cool, dry place. Use as you would any commercial mix.

Biscuit Mix No. 3

6 cups	sifted pastry flour or 5 1/4 cups (1.3 L) all-purpose flour	1.5 L
3 tbsp	baking powder	45 mL
1 1/2 tsp	salt	7 mL
1 cup	shortening (8 oz [250 g])	250 mL

1. In a large bowl, sift together flour, baking powder and salt 2 or 3 times to distribute evenly. Cut in shortening until mixture resembles coarse crumbs.

2. Store mix in an airtight tin or jar. Makes about 7 1/2 to 8 cups (1.875 to 2 L) and will keep 4 to 6 weeks at room temperature.

Oat or Bran Muffins

1	egg	1
2 tbsp	vegetable oil *or* shortening, melted	25 mL
1 cup	soured skim milk	250 mL
1/2 tsp	baking soda	2 mL
2/3 cup	All-Bran cereal *or* rolled oats	150 mL
1 1/3 cups	homemade or packaged biscuit mix	325 mL
1/3 cup	packed brown sugar	75 mL

Preheat oven to 400° F (200° C)
Muffin tin, greased

1. In a large bowl, beat egg. Add oil, milk, baking soda and All-Bran, mixing well. Add Biscuit Mix and brown sugar.

2. Spoon batter into prepared muffin tin, filling cups two-thirds full. Bake in preheated oven for 18 to 20 minutes.

VARIATION

🧁 **Orange Muffins:** Add a little grated orange zest, plus 2 to 3 tbsp (25 to 45 mL) sugar for a sweeter muffin.

HINT: Use a packaged muffin mix, or one of your homemade mix recipes, to make a good quick coffee cake. Bake in a square pan and top with cinnamon and sugar.

Bran and Whole-Wheat Mix

3 cups	whole-wheat flour	750 mL
3 cups	all-purpose flour	750 mL
2 1/2 cups	whole-bran cereal	625 mL
1 1/2 cups	non-fat dry milk	375 mL
1 1/2 cups	packed brown sugar *or* granulated sugar	375 mL
4 tbsp	baking powder	60 mL
1 tbsp	salt	15 mL
1 1/2 cups	shortening	375 mL

1. In a large bowl, using a pastry blender or your fingers, mix together whole-wheat flour, all-purpose flour, cereal, dry milk, brown sugar, baking powder, salt and shortening. Blend well until mixture resembles fine crumbs.

2. Store mix in an airtight container in a cool, dry place for up to 3 months. Makes 12 cups (3 L).

Nutty Bran and Whole-Wheat Muffins

4 1/2 cups	BRAN AND WHOLE-WHEAT MIX (see recipe above)	1.125 L
1 1/4 cups	water	300 mL
1	egg, slightly beaten	1
1/2 cup	chopped nuts	125 mL

Preheat oven to 400° F (200° C)
Muffin tin, greased

1. In a large bowl, combine mix, water, egg and nuts. Stir just to moisten.

2. Spoon batter into prepared muffin tin. Bake in preheated oven for 15 to 20 minutes or until toothpick inserted in center comes out clean and dry.

Cinnamon Raisin Bran Muffin Mix

6 cups	all-purpose flour	1.5 L
4 cups	raisins	1 L
3 cups	Bran Flakes cereal	750 mL
3 cups	wheat bran	750 mL
2 cups	packed brown sugar	500 mL
2 tbsp	baking soda	25 mL
2 tbsp	cinnamon	25 mL
2 tsp	salt	10 mL

1. In a large bowl combine flour, raisins, cereal, bran, brown sugar, baking soda, cinnamon and salt.

2. Store mix in an airtight container in a cool, dry place for up to 4 weeks. Makes about 13 1/2 cups (3.375 L).

Breakfast Muffins

2 1/4 cups	CINNAMON RAISIN BRAN MIX (see recipe above)	550 mL
1/2 cup	low-fat plain yogurt	125 mL
1/2 cup	milk	125 mL
3 tbsp	vegetable oil	45 mL

Preheat oven to 400° F (200° C)
6-cup muffin tin, greased or paper-lined

1. Put muffin mix in a large bowl. In another bowl, whisk together yogurt, milk and oil. Stir into mix just until moistened.

2. Spoon batter into prepared muffin tin, filling cups to the top. Bake in preheated oven for 20 to 25 minutes or until firm to the touch.

Corn Muffin Mix

4 cups	all-purpose flour	1 L
4 cups	cornmeal	1 L
2 cups	non-fat dry milk	500 mL
3/4 cup	granulated sugar	175 mL
1/4 cup	double-acting baking powder	50 mL
1 tbsp	salt	15 mL

1. In a large bowl, combine flour, cornmeal, milk, sugar, baking powder and salt. Mix with your hands, lifting mixture and letting it fall through your fingers.
2. Store mix in an airtight container in a cool, dry place. Makes 9 1/2 cups (2.375 L).

Corn Muffins

1	egg	1
1 cup	water	250 mL
2 1/3 cups	CORN MUFFIN MIX (see recipe above)	575 mL
1/4 cup	butter or margarine, melted *or* bacon or sausage fat	50 mL

Preheat oven to 425° F (220° C)
12-cup muffin tin, greased

1. In a bowl with a fork mix together egg and water until blended. Add Corn Muffin Mix and melted butter, stirring just to blend.
2. Spoon batter evenly into prepared muffin tin. Bake in preheated oven for 20 minutes or until golden brown.

HINT: To check baking powder for freshness, stir 1 tsp (5 mL) baking powder into 1/2 cup (125 mL) boiling water. If the mixture does not fizz and bubble, the baking powder has lost its leavening power and should be thrown out.

Granola Mix

4 cups	quick or old-fashioned rolled oats	1 L
1 cup	coarsely chopped walnuts	250 mL
3/4 cup	hulled sunflower seeds	175 mL
1/2 cup	slivered almonds	125 mL
1/2 cup	coarsely chopped pecans	125 mL
1/2 cup	wheat germ	125 mL
1/2 cup	natural wheat and barley cereal	125 mL
1/3 cup	sesame seeds	75 mL
1 1/2 cups	shredded coconut	375 mL
1 cup	packed light brown sugar	250 mL
2/3 cup	vegetable oil	150 mL
2/3 cup	water	150 mL
1/2 cup	honey	125 mL
2 tsp	vanilla	10 mL
1 tsp	cinnamon	5 mL
1/2 tsp	ground nutmeg	2 mL
1 1/2 cups	raisins	375 mL

Preheat oven to 300° F (150° C)
Two large roasting pans

1. In a large bowl, combine oats, walnuts, sunflower seeds, almonds, pecans, wheat germ, cereal, sesame seeds and coconut. Set aside.

2. In a large saucepan over low heat, combine brown sugar, oil, water, honey, vanilla, cinnamon and nutmeg. Heat, stirring occasionally, for 15 to 20 minutes or until sugar dissolves. Do not allow to boil. Pour over dry ingredients and stir until well coated.

3. Divide batter evenly between the 2 pans. Bake in preheated oven for 25 to 30 minutes (or 10 minutes more if you want a crunchier texture). Set aside to cool.

4. When cool, break into pieces. Stir in raisins. Store mix in airtight containers in a cool, dry place for up to 6 months. Makes about 14 cups (3.5 L) mix.

Granola Muffins

1 cup	MULTIPURPOSE MIX, (preferably Whole-Wheat [page 92])	250 mL
1/2 cup + 2 tbsp	GRANOLA MIX (see recipe above)	125 mL + 25 mL
2 tbsp	packed light brown sugar	25 mL
1/2 cup	milk	125 mL
1	egg, slightly beaten	1

Preheat oven to 400° F (200° C)
6-cup muffin tin, greased

1. In a large bowl, combine Multipurpose Mix, 1/2 cup (125 mL) Granola Mix and sugar. Add milk and egg, stirring just until moistened.

2. Spoon batter into prepared muffin tin, filling cups two-thirds full. Sprinkle tops with remaining 2 tbsp (25 mL) Granola mix. Bake in preheated oven for 20 to 25 minutes or until golden brown.

Just-a-Minute Mix

10 cups	all-purpose flour	2.5 L
1/3 cup	baking powder	75 mL
1 tbsp	salt	15 mL
2 1/3 cups	shortening (1 lb [500 g])	575 mL

A quick and easy recipe that really just takes a minute!

1. In a large mixing bowl, combine flour, baking powder and salt, mixing well. With a pastry blender or 2 knives, cut in shortening until mixture resembles coarse crumbs.

2. Store mix in an airtight container in a cool, dry place. Makes about 16 cups (4 L).

Just-a-Minute Muffins

2 1/2 cups	JUST-A-MINUTE MIX (see recipe above)	625 mL
3 tbsp	granulated sugar	45 mL
3/4 cup	milk	175 mL
1	egg, beaten	1

Preheat oven to 400° F (200° C)
12-cup muffin tin, greased

1. In a large bowl, combine mix and sugar. Add milk and egg, stirring just until moistened. Batter will be lumpy.

2. Spoon batter into prepared muffin tin. Bake in preheated oven for 20 to 25 minutes.

NOTE: You can add raisins, blueberries or any other fruits, as well as chocolate chips — whatever you have on hand.

HINT: If you have saved egg yolks from previous recipes, use them in place of whole eggs. Use 2 yolks for every whole egg.

Multipurpose Mix

10 cups	all-purpose flour	2.5 L
1/2 cup	granulated sugar	125 mL
1/3 cup	baking powder	75 mL
1 tbsp	salt	15 mL
2 cups	shortening	500 mL

1. In a large bowl, combine flour, sugar, baking powder and salt, mixing well. With a pastry blender or 2 knives, cut in shortening until mixture resembles coarse crumbs.

2. Store in an airtight container in a cool, dry place for up to 3 months. Makes about 13 cups (3.25 L).

VARIATION

Whole-Wheat Multipurpose Mix: Use 5 cups (1.25 L) all-purpose flour and 5 cups (1.25 L) whole-wheat flour.

Cornmeal Muffins

1 1/2 cups	MULTIPURPOSE MIX (see recipe above)	375 mL
3/4 cup	cornmeal	175 mL
2 tbsp	granulated sugar	25 mL
1 cup	milk	250 mL
1	egg, slightly beaten	1

Preheat oven to 400° F (200° C)
12-cup muffin tin, greased

1. In a bowl combine mix, cornmeal and sugar. Add milk and egg, stirring just until moistened.

2. Spoon batter into prepared muffin tin. Bake in preheated oven for 25 to 30 minutes.

Rolled Oats Mix

4 cups	all-purpose flour	1 L
4 cups	quick-cooking oats (not instant)	1 L
1 1/2 cups	dry non-fat milk	375 mL
4 tbsp	double-acting baking powder	60 mL
1 tbsp	salt	15 mL
1 1/2 cups	solid vegetable shortening	375 mL

1. In a large bowl, combine flour, oats, milk, baking powder and salt. With a pastry blender, cut in shortening until mixture resembles coarse crumbs.

2. Store in an airtight container and keep in a cool, dry place. Makes about 10 cups (2.5 L).

Oat Muffins

2 1/4 cups	ROLLED OATS MIX (see recipe above)	550 mL
1/4 cup	raisins (optional)	50 mL
2 tbsp	granulated sugar	25 mL
2/3 cup	water	150 mL
1	egg, beaten	1

Preheat oven to 425° F (220° C)
12-cup muffin tin, greased

1. In a large bowl, combine mix, raisins (if using), sugar, water and egg. Stir just until moistened. Do not overmix.

2. Spoon batter into prepared muffin tin. Bake in preheated oven for about 20 minutes.

Whole-Wheat Mix

4 cups	whole-wheat flour	1 L
4 cups	all-purpose flour	1 L
1 1/2 cups	non-fat dry milk	375 mL
1 1/2 cups	granulated sugar	375 mL
1/2 cup	wheat germ	125 mL
4 tbsp	double-acting baking powder	50 mL
1 tbsp	salt	15 mL
1 1/2 cups	solid vegetable shortening	375 mL

1. In a large bowl, combine whole-wheat flour, all-purpose flour, milk, sugar, wheat germ, baking powder and salt. With a pastry blender or 2 knives, cut in shortening until mixture is crumbly.

2. Store mix in an airtight container in a cool, dry place. Makes about 14 cups (3.5 L).

Whole-Wheat Muffins

1	egg	1
1 1/4 cups	water	300 mL
4 1/2 cups	WHOLE-WHEAT MIX (see recipe above)	1.125 L

Preheat oven to 400° F (200° C)
12-cup muffin tin, greased

1. In a large bowl, beat egg slightly with water. Stir in mix just until moistened.

2. Spoon batter into prepared muffin tin. Bake in preheated oven for 15 to 20 minutes.

Bacon Muffins

2 cups	homemade or packaged biscuit mix	500 mL
2 tbsp	granulated sugar	25 mL
1	egg	1
2/3 cup	cold water *or* milk	150 mL
6	slices bacon, fried crisp and crumbled (about 1/4 cup [50 mL])	6

Preheat oven to 400° F (200° C)
12-cup muffin tin, greased

1. In a large bowl, combine biscuit mix, sugar, egg and water. With a fork, beat vigorously for 1 minute. Stir in bacon, mixing just until blended.

2. Spoon batter into prepared muffin tin, filling cups two-thirds full. Bake in preheated oven for 15 minutes.

Quick Banana Muffins

4 cups	homemade or packaged biscuit mix	1 L
1 cup	granulated sugar	250 mL
1/2 cup	all-purpose flour	125 mL
1/2 tsp	baking soda	2 mL
4	eggs, beaten	4
1 cup	sour cream	250 mL
2 cups	mashed ripe bananas (about 4 medium)	500 mL
1 cup	chopped walnuts	250 mL

Preheat oven to 400° F (200° C)
Muffin tin, greased

1. In a large bowl, combine biscuit mix, sugar, flour and baking soda.

2. In another bowl, combine eggs and sour cream. Stir into dry ingredients. Add mashed banana and fold in chopped nuts.

3. Spoon batter into prepared muffin tin, filling cups three-quarters full. Bake in preheated oven for 15 to 20 minutes or until toothpick inserted in center comes out clean.

HINT: To shell walnuts, soak overnight in salt water before gently cracking. This will remove the nutmeat intact.

Blueberry Cornbread Muffins

1	pkg blueberry muffin mix (such as Duncan Hines)	1
1 cup	yellow cornmeal	250 mL
1 cup	water	250 mL
1	egg	1

Preheat oven to 400° F (200° C)
Muffin tin, greased or paper-lined

1. In a large bowl, combine mix and cornmeal.
2. In another bowl, mix together water and egg. Add to the dry ingredients, blending with a fork just until moistened. Fold in packaged blueberries.
3. Spoon batter into prepared muffin tin, filling cups three-quarters full. Bake in preheated oven for 20 to 25 minutes.

Blueberry Pancake Muffins

2 cups	pancake mix	500 mL
1/2 cup	granulated sugar *or* packed brown sugar	125 mL
2	eggs, beaten	2
1 cup	milk	250 mL
1/2 cup	butter or margarine, melted	125 mL

Preheat oven to 400° F (200° C)
Muffin tin, paper-lined

1. In a large bowl, combine pancake mix and sugar. Add eggs, milk and melted butter. Stir just to moisten, but do not overmix.
2. Spoon batter into prepared muffin tin. Bake in preheated oven for 15 to 20 minutes or until golden brown.

For something a little different, let's take a muffin mix and turn it into delicious cookies.

Blueberry Cinnamon Treats

1	pkg wild blueberry muffin mix (such as Betty Crocker)	1
2 tbsp	vegetable oil	25 mL
2 tbsp	milk	25 mL
1/2 tsp	cinnamon	2 mL
1	egg	1
LEMON BUTTER FROSTING		
1 1/2 cups	icing sugar	375 mL
2 tbsp	softened butter or margarine	25 mL
1/2 tsp	lemon zest	2 mL
1 tsp	lemon juice	5 mL
1 tbsp	milk	15 mL

Preheat oven to 375° F (190° C)
Cookie sheet

1. In a large bowl, combine muffin mix, oil, milk, cinnamon and egg. Fold in packaged blueberries.

2. Drop dough by teaspoonfuls (5 mL), 2 inches (5 cm) apart onto ungreased cookie sheet. Bake in preheated oven for 10 minutes or until edges are golden brown. Remove from cookie sheet immediately.

3. In a bowl mix together icing sugar and butter. Stir in lemon zest and lemon juice. Then add milk 1 tsp (5 mL) at a time until desired consistency is reached. Frost cookies and serve.

Blueberry Miniatures

2 cups	homemade or packaged biscuit mix	500 mL
1 tbsp	granulated sugar	15 mL
1	egg	1
2 tbsp	butter or margarine, melted	25 mL
3/4 cup	milk	175 mL
1 cup	blueberries, washed and stemmed	250 mL
1 tbsp	SUGAR-CINNAMON MIX (page 179)	15 mL

Preheat oven to 400° F (200° C)
Miniature muffin tin, greased

1. In a large bowl, combine biscuit mix and sugar.

2. In another bowl, beat egg slightly. Stir in melted butter and milk. Add to biscuit mixture all at once and stir just until moistened. Fold in blueberries.

3. Spoon batter into prepared muffin tin. Sprinkle with Sugar-Cinnamon Mix. Bake in preheated oven for 10 minutes or until golden brown. Remove from pans and serve hot.

Blueberry Nut Muffins

1	egg	1
1/2 cup	milk	125 mL
1	pkg wild blueberry muffin mix	1
1/2 cup	chopped nuts	125 mL

Preheat oven to 400° F (200° C)
12-cup muffin tin, greased or paper-lined

1. In a large bowl, blend together egg and milk. Stir in muffin mix just until blended. Batter should be lumpy. Fold in packaged blueberries and nuts.

2. Spoon batter into prepared muffin tin. Bake in preheated oven for 15 to 20 minutes.

Frosted Brownie Fudge Muffins

1	pkg hot fudge brownie mix (such as Betty Crocker)	1
1/2 cup	creamy chocolate frosting	125 mL
1/2 cup	whipped cream	125 mL

Preheat oven to 350° F (180° C)
6-cup muffin tin, greased

1. Prepare brownie mix according to package instructions. Spoon half the batter into prepared muffin tin.

2. Before opening hot fudge pouch, squeeze until fudge is softened, about 20 to 25 times. Squeeze fudge evenly over batter in cups. Spoon remaining batter over fudge. Bake in preheated oven for about 25 to 30 minutes. Set aside to cool slightly.

3. Warm frosting in microwave on High for 30 seconds. Drizzle over warm muffins and top with whipped cream.

Easy Buttermilk Muffins

1 cup	buttermilk baking mix	250 mL
3 tbsp	granulated sugar	45 mL
1	egg	1
1/3 cup	water	75 mL

Preheat oven to 400° F (200° C)
Muffin tin, greased or paper-lined

1. In a large bowl, combine buttermilk mix, sugar, egg and water. Whisk together for about 30 seconds.

2. Spoon batter into prepared muffin tin, filling cups three-quarters full. Bake in preheated oven for 15 to 20 minutes.

VARIATIONS

🧁 **Buttermilk Nut Muffins:** Add 1/4 cup (50 mL) chopped nuts.

🧁 **Buttermilk Date Muffins:** Add 1/4 cup (50 mL) chopped dates.

Buttermilk Corn Muffins

1/2 cup	buttermilk mix	125 mL
1/2 cup	yellow cornmeal	125 mL
2 tbsp	granulated sugar	25 mL
1	egg	1
1/4 tsp	salt	50 mL
1/3 cup	water	75 mL
2 tbsp	butter, melted	25 mL

Preheat oven to 400° F (200° C)
Muffin tin, greased or paper-lined

1. In a medium bowl, combine buttermilk mix, cornmeal, sugar, egg, salt and water. Mix in melted butter, blending well.

2. Spoon batter into prepared muffin tin, filling cups three-quarters full. Bake in preheated oven for 15 to 20 minutes.

Cheddar Beer Muffins

3 cups	homemade or packaged biscuit mix	750 mL
1/4 cup	granulated sugar	50 mL
1	egg	1
3/4 cup + 1/3 cup	milk	175 mL + 75 mL
2 tbsp	beer	25 mL
1/2 cup	grated Cheddar cheese	125 mL

Preheat oven to 400° F (200° C)
Muffin tin, greased or paper-lined

1. In a large bowl, combine biscuit mix and sugar. Stir with a fork until no lumps remain.

2. In another bowl, whisk together egg, milk and beer. Pour into dry ingredients. Add cheese, stirring just until moistened. Do not overmix.

3. Spoon batter into prepared muffin tin, filling cups three-quarters full. Bake in preheated oven for 12 to 15 minutes.

NOTE: If desired, increase the beer to 1/3 cup (75 mL).

Chive Dinner Muffins

2 cups	homemade or packaged biscuit mix	500 mL
2 tbsp	shortening	25 mL
1	egg	1
2/3 cup	milk or water	150 mL
1/4 cup	snipped chives	50 mL

Preheat oven to 400° F (200° C)
12-cup muffin tin, greased

1. In a bowl with a fork, combine mix, shortening, egg, milk and chives. Beat vigorously for 1 minute.

2. Spoon batter into prepared muffin tin, filling cups three-quarters full. Bake in preheated oven for 15 minutes.

Quick Cocoa Bran Muffins

1	pkg bran and honey muffin mix	1
1/4 cup	cocoa	50 mL
1	egg, slightly beaten	1
3/4 cup	water	175 mL
1/2 cup	raisins	125 mL
1/4 cup	finely chopped nuts (optional)	50 mL

Preheat oven to 400° F (200° C)
Muffin tin, greased or paper-lined

1. In a large bowl, combine muffin mix and cocoa, blending well. Stir in egg and water just until blended. Add raisins and, if using, nuts.

2. Spoon batter into prepared muffin tin, filling cups three-quarters full. Bake in preheated oven for 15 to 17 minutes. Serve warm.

Bacon, Chive and Corn Muffins

1	pkg (12 oz [340 g]) corn muffin mix	1
2 tsp	minced fresh chives or dried chives	10 mL
Dash	black pepper	Dash
1	egg	1
2/3 cup	milk	150 mL
1/2 cup	crumbled crisp bacon	125 mL

Preheat oven to 400° F (200° C)
12-cup muffin tin, greased

1. In a large bowl, combine corn muffin mix, chives and pepper. Add egg and milk and mix according to package directions. Fold in bacon.

2. Spoon batter into prepared muffin tin. Bake in preheated oven for 15 to 20 minutes. Serve hot.

Double Corn Muffins

1	pkg (12 oz [340 g]) corn muffin mix	1
1	can (16 oz [473 mL]) whole kernel corn, drained	1
1	can (2 1/4 oz [64 g]) deviled ham	1

Preheat oven to 375° F (190° C)
Muffin tin, greased or paper-lined

1. Prepare muffin mix according to package directions. Stir in corn.

2. Spoon batter into prepared muffin tin, filling cups two-thirds full. Drop a spoonful of deviled ham in center of each muffin. Bake in preheated oven for 20 minutes.

Spicy Corn Muffins

2	eggs	2
3/4 cup	milk	175 mL
2	pkgs (each 8 1/2 oz [251 mL]) corn muffin mix	2
1 cup	shredded Cheddar cheese	250 mL
1 cup	thawed frozen corn	250 mL
1/4 cup	drained sliced jalapeño peppers	50 mL

Preheat oven to 400° F (200° C)
Muffin tin, greased or paper-lined

1. In a small bowl, lightly beat together eggs and milk.

2. In a large bowl, combine muffin mix, cheese, corn and peppers. Stir in milk mixture and stir just until blended. Batter will be lumpy. Let stand for 5 minutes.

3. Spoon batter into prepared muffin tin, filling cups to the top. Bake in preheated oven for 20 minutes or until golden brown.

Creamy Cottage Cheese Muffins

1/3 cup	granulated sugar	75 mL
3 tbsp	butter *or* margarine	45 mL
1/2 cup	cream-style cottage cheese	125 mL
1 tsp	grated lemon zest	5 mL
1	egg	1
1 3/4 cups	homemade or packaged biscuit mix	425 mL
1/2 cup	milk	125 mL

Preheat oven to 400° F (200° C)
Muffin tin, greased or paper-lined

1. In a large bowl, cream together sugar and butter. Beat in cottage cheese and lemon zest. Add egg, beating well. Stir in biscuit mix and milk just until moistened.

2. Spoon batter into prepared muffin tin, filling cups three-quarters full. Bake in preheated oven for 20 minutes.

HINT: When you are creaming butter and sugar together, it is a good idea to rinse the bowl with boiling water first. They will cream faster.

Festive Cranberry Date Muffins

3/4 cup	chopped almonds, pecans or walnuts	175 mL
1	pkg date and orange loaf and muffin mix	1
1/2 cup	milk	125 mL
2	eggs, lightly beaten	2
3 tbsp	butter, melted	45 mL
1 cup	fresh or frozen cranberries, cut in half	250 mL

Preheat oven to 350° F (180° C)
Muffin tin, greased or paper-lined

1. Toast nuts in preheated oven for 5 minutes or until slightly browned. Set aside.

2. Into a large bowl, pour muffin mix and make a well in the center. Add milk, eggs and butter, stirring just until blended. Fold in nuts and cranberries.

3. Spoon batter into prepared muffin tin, filling cups three-quarters full. Bake in preheated oven for 15 to 20 minutes or until a toothpick inserted in center comes out clean and dry.

Devil's Food Muffins

1	pkg devil's food cake mix	1
3	eggs	3
1 1/3 cups	water	325 mL
1/2 cup	vegetable oil	125 mL

Preheat oven to 400° F (200° C)
Muffin tin, paper-lined

1. Into a large bowl, pour cake mix and make a well in the center.

2. In another bowl, with a mixing spoon, beat together eggs, water and oil. Add to cake mix and stir just until moistened.

3. Spoon batter into prepared muffin tin, filling cups to the top. Bake in preheated oven for 15 to 20 minutes.

NOTE: For an extra special treat, ice muffin tops with vanilla or chocolate icing, or put vanilla icing on half of muffin top and chocolate on the other half.

Fruit Muffin Buns

2 cups	buttermilk baking mix	500 mL
1 tbsp	granulated sugar	15 mL
1/8 tsp	ground nutmeg	0.5 mL
3/4 cup	milk	175 mL
1/2 cup	softened butter or margarine	125 mL
	Fruit pie filling or stewed fruit, drained	

Preheat oven to 375° F (190° C)
12-cup muffin tin, greased

1. In a large bowl, combine buttermilk mix, sugar and nutmeg. Add milk and stir until mixture stiffens. Turn out on a floured board and roll out to 1/8 inch (2 mm) thick.

2. Spread with 1/4 cup (50 mL) butter. Fold dough in half and spread with remaining butter. Fold again and roll into a rectangle. Cut into twelve 3-inch (7.5 cm) squares.

3. Place squares in prepared muffin tin. Spoon in fruit filling. Pull corners of dough together and pinch to seal. Bake in preheated oven for 25 minutes.

VARIATION

🧁 **Dried Fruit Filling:** Cook, drain and chop 6 dried apricots, 3 dried prunes and 1 dried peach. Set aside. In a bowl beat together 1 egg, 1/2 cup (125 mL) sugar, 1 tsp (5 mL) lemon juice and 1/2 tsp (2 mL) cinnamon. Stir in fruit.

Grandma's Muffins

2 cups	pancake and waffle mix	500 mL
1/2 cup	lightly packed brown sugar	125 mL
1 tsp	cinnamon	5 mL
3/4 cup	milk	175 mL
1 tsp	vanilla	5 mL
1	egg, slightly beaten	1
1/4 cup	vegetable oil	50 mL
3/4 cup	raisins (optional)	175 mL

1. In a large bowl, mix together pancake mix, brown sugar and cinnamon.

2. In another bowl, combine milk, vanilla, egg and oil. Stir into dry ingredients just until blended. If using, fold in raisins.

3. Spoon batter into prepared muffin tin, dividing evenly. Bake in preheated oven for 18 to 20 minutes.

Ham and Cheddar Muffins

2 cups	homemade or packaged biscuit mix	500 mL
2 tsp	dry mustard *or* 2 tbsp (25 mL) granulated sugar	10 mL
1	egg, beaten	1
1/2 cup	milk	125 mL
1	can (6.5 oz [184 g]) flaked ham	1
1 1/2 cups	grated Cheddar cheese	375 mL

Preheat oven to 400° F (200° C)
12-cup muffin tin, greased or paper-lined

1. In a medium bowl with a fork, combine mix, dry mustard, egg and milk. Stir in ham and cheese just until blended.

2. Spoon batter into prepared muffin tin, dividing evenly. Bake in preheated oven for about 20 minutes.

Hawaiian Hula Muffins

2 cups	homemade or packaged biscuit mix	500 mL
3/4 cup	finely crushed hard candies, butterscotch-flavored	175 mL
3/4 cup	milk	175 mL
1/4 cup	vegetable oil	50 mL
1 cup	sour cream	250 mL
1	can (13 1/2 oz [385 g]) crushed pineapple, drained	1

Preheat oven to 350° F (180° C)
8-cup muffin tin, greased or paper-lined

1. In a bowl combine biscuit mix and 1/4 cup (50 mL) of the candy.

2. In a small bowl, combine milk and oil. Add to biscuit mixture, stirring just until moistened.

3. Spoon batter into prepared muffin tin. Bake in preheated oven for 10 to 12 minutes.

4. Split warm muffins and spread bottom sections with half the sour cream. Spoon on half the pineapple and half the remaining candy. Replace muffin tops and cover with remaining sour cream, pineapple and candy.

HINT: Use reserved juice from drained pineapple to retain the bright fresh coloring of sliced apples, bananas, avocados and mushrooms. The juice prevents darkening without adding an overpowering flavor.

Marmalade Breakfast Muffins

2 1/4 cups	buttermilk baking mix	550 mL
2 tbsp	granulated sugar	25 mL
1	egg, slightly beaten	1
1/2 tsp	vanilla	2 mL
1/4 cup	all-fruit orange marmalade spread	50 mL

Preheat oven to 400° F (200° C)
Muffin tin, greased or paper-lined

1. In a large bowl, combine buttermilk mix and sugar. Add egg and vanilla, mixing just until blended.

2. Spoon batter into prepared muffin tin, filling cups half full. Top each with 1 tsp (5 mL) orange marmalade. Spoon remaining batter evenly over marmalade. Bake in preheated oven for 12 to 15 minutes or until a toothpick inserted in center comes out clean.

NOTE: In place of the egg, you can use 1/4 cup (50 mL) egg substitute plus 1 cup (250 mL) water.

Meal-in-One Muffin

1 tbsp	butter *or* margarine	15 mL
2 tbsp	finely chopped onion	25 mL
2 tbsp	finely chopped celery	25 mL
2 tbsp	shredded carrot	25 mL
1	can (4 1/2 oz [128 mL]) deviled ham	1
2 cups	packaged or homemade biscuit mix	500 mL
1 tbsp	granulated sugar	15 mL
1/2 cup	shredded Cheddar cheese	125 mL
1	egg	1
2/3 cup	milk	150 mL

Preheat oven to 400° F (200° C)
Muffin tin, greased or paper-lined

1. In a small frying pan, heat butter over medium heat. Add onion, celery and carrot, cooking until tender but not brown. Allow to cool. Stir in ham and set aside.

2. In a medium bowl, combine biscuit mix, sugar, cheese, egg and milk. Beat with a fork for 1 minute. Spoon into prepared muffin tin, filling cups two-thirds full.

3. Make an indentation in center of each and spoon in ham mixture. Bake in preheated oven for 18 to 20 minutes or until browned.

Quick n' Easy Oatmeal Raisin Muffins

2 cups	buttermilk baking mix	500 mL
1/2 cup	quick-cooking rolled oats (not instant)	125 mL
1/2 cup	raisins	125 mL
2 tbsp	granulated sugar	25 mL
1	egg	1
2/3 cup	milk	150 mL
	Butter or margarine	

Preheat oven to 400° F (200° C)
Muffin tin, greased or paper-lined

1. In a large bowl, combine buttermilk mix, oats, raisins and sugar.

2. In another bowl, beat together egg and milk. Pour into dry ingredients and stir until well blended.

3. Spoon batter into prepared muffin tin, filling cups three-quarters full. Bake in preheated oven for 15 minutes.

NOTE: These muffins are delicious served warm. Split them and spread with butter or any other favorites.

Crunchy Onion Muffins

3 cups	homemade or packaged biscuit mix	750 mL
1 tsp	onion salt	5 mL
3/4 cup	shredded Cheddar cheese	175 mL
1	can (3 1/2 oz [100 mL]) french fried onion rings, crumbled	1
1 cup	milk	250 mL
1	egg	1

Preheat oven to 400° F (200° C)
Muffin tin, greased or paper-lined

1. In a large bowl, combine biscuit mix, onion salt, cheese, crumbled onion rings, milk and egg. Mix until well blended, but do not overmix.

2. Spoon batter into prepared muffin tin, filling cups to the top. Bake in preheated oven for 15 minutes or until golden brown.

HINT: If you shake an egg and you hear a rattle, the egg is most likely bad. Don't use it.

Glazed Orange Muffins

1	pkg bran with fruit and muffin mix (such as Duncan Hines)	1
1	egg	1
1 1/2 cups	water	375 mL
1/4 cup	orange marmalade	50 mL
GLAZE		
1/3 cup	orange juice	75 mL
1/4 cup	granulated sugar	50 mL
1 tbsp	grated orange zest	15 mL

Preheat oven to 400° F (200° C)
12-cup muffin tin, greased or paper-lined

1. In a bowl combine muffin mix, egg and water, mixing well.

2. Spoon just enough batter into prepared tin to cover bottoms. Add 1 tsp (5 mL) marmalade to each. Fill with remaining batter. Bake in preheated oven for about 20 minutes.

3. In a small saucepan over low heat, combine orange juice, sugar and zest. Cook until sugar dissolves.

4. Place warm muffins on a rack with waxed paper underneath. Drizzle hot glaze over muffins.

Orange Date Nut Muffins

1	pkg date-and-orange loaf cake mix (such as Robin Hood)	1
2	eggs	2
1 cup	sour cream	250 mL
2 tbsp	vegetable oil	25 mL
1/2 cup	chopped nuts	125 mL
1/4 cup	lightly packed brown sugar	50 mL
1/4 cup	chopped nuts	50 mL

Preheat oven to 375° F (190° C)
Muffin tin, greased or paper-lined

1. In a large bowl, combine cake mix, eggs, sour cream, oil and nuts. Mix together just until moistened and blended.

2. Spoon batter into prepared muffin tin, filling cups three-quarters full. Sprinkle with brown sugar and chopped nuts. Bake in preheated oven for 20 to 25 minutes.

Deluxe Pizza Muffins

2 cups	homemade or packaged biscuit mix	500 mL
3/4 cup	milk	175 mL
FILLING		
1	jar (15 1/2 oz [458 mL]) spaghetti sauce	1
1	can (4 oz [115 g]) sliced mushrooms, drained	1
1	small green pepper, chopped	1
1	pkg (3 oz [75 g]) sliced pepperoni, cut into quarters	1
1 cup	shredded Mozzarella cheese	250 mL

Preheat oven to 400° F (200° C)
12-cup muffin tin, sprayed with vegetable spray

1. In a bowl blend together biscuit mix and milk to form a soft dough. Turn out onto a floured surface and knead about 20 times. Roll dough into a rectangle, about 1/8 inch (2 mm) thick. With a cookie cutter or inverted glass, cut out twelve 4-inch (10 cm) circles. Press the circles into bottom and up sides of muffin cups.

2. In a large bowl combine spaghetti sauce, mushrooms, green pepper and pepperoni. Spoon over dough circles and then sprinkle with cheese. Bake in preheated oven for 15 minutes or until browned.

Polka Dot Muffins

1 cup	chopped fresh cranberries *or* frozen cranberries, thawed	250 mL
1/2 cup	granulated sugar	125 mL
1 tsp	grated orange zest	5 mL
1	egg, beaten	1
1/4 cup	granulated sugar	50 mL
1/2 cup	orange juice	125 mL
2 tbsp	vegetable oil	25 mL
2 cups	homemade or packaged biscuit mix	500 mL

Preheat oven to 400° F (200° C)
Muffin tin, greased or paper-lined

1. In a bowl combine cranberries, 1/2 cup (125 mL) sugar and orange zest. Set aside.

2. In another bowl, combine egg, 1/4 cup (50 mL) sugar, orange juice and oil. Add biscuit mix and stir just until moistened. Fold in cranberry mixture.

3. Spoon batter into prepared muffin tin, filling cups three-quarters full. Bake in preheated oven for 25 minutes or until browned.

HINT: Try this for a quick and easy supper. Kids, especially, will love it!

Muffin-Tin Supper: Grease 2 large size muffin pans. Fill one with corn muffin mix and prepare as directed on the package. Fill the other with corned-beef hash. Make an indentation in center of hash mound and drop an egg into it. Bake at temperature recommended for muffins.

Raspberry Buttermilk Balls

1	pkg buttermilk baking mix	1
	Raspberry jam	

Preheat oven to 450° F (230° C)
10- to 12-cup muffin tin

1. Prepare baking mix as directed on package. Roll out dough to 1/2 inch (1 cm) thick. With a floured cookie cutter or inverted glass, cut into 10 to 12 circles. Reserve remaining dough. Place a circle in each muffin cup.

2. Make a depression in center of each cup of batter. Fill each with 1 tsp (5 mL) raspberry jam.

3. Shape remaining dough into 10 to 12 balls and place on top of jam. Bake in preheated oven for 10 minutes or until lightly browned.

Sesame Cheese Muffins

1 1/2 cups	homemade or packaged biscuit mix	375 mL
1 cup	shredded sharp processed cheese	250 mL
1 tbsp	vegetable oil	15 mL
1/2 cup	chopped onions	125 mL
1	egg, beaten	1
1/2 cup	milk	125 mL
1 tbsp	toasted sesame seeds	15 mL
2 tbsp	butter or margarine, melted	25 mL

Preheat oven to 400° F (200° C)
Muffin tin, greased or paper-lined

1. In a large bowl, combine biscuit mix and half of the cheese.

2. In a small skillet, heat oil over medium heat. Cook onions just until tender.

3. In a bowl combine egg, milk and onions. Add all at once to biscuit mixture and stir just until moistened.

4. Spoon batter into prepared muffin tin, filling cups three-quarters full. Sprinkle with remaining cheese and sesame seeds. Drizzle melted butter over top. Bake in preheated oven for 15 to 20 minutes.

Stuffed Bacon Cheese Muffins

2 cups	homemade or packaged biscuit mix	500 mL
5	slices bacon, cooked crisp and crumbled	5
3/4 cup	milk	175 mL
1	egg, beaten	1
12	cubes (1/2 inch [1 cm]) Swiss cheese	12

Preheat oven to 400° F (200° C)
12-cup muffin tin, greased

1. In a bowl combine biscuit mix and bacon. Add milk and egg, stirring just until blended.

2. Spoon half of the batter evenly into prepared muffin tin. Add a cheese cube to each and top with remaining batter. Bake in preheated oven for 25 minutes or until golden brown. Serve hot.

Wheat Germ Muffins

2 cups	Wheat Germ Pancake Mix	500 mL
1/2 cup	margarine	125 mL
1/2 cup	granulated sugar	125 mL
1	large egg	1
1 1/4 cups	milk	300 mL

Preheat oven to 375° F (190° C)
Muffin tin, greased or paper-lined

1. Into a large bowl, pour pancake mix. With a pastry blender, cut in margarine until mixture resembles coarse crumbs. Add sugar.

2. In another bowl, beat egg. Add milk and beat well. Pour into dry ingredients and stir slowly, just until moistened and blended. Batter should be lumpy.

3. Spoon batter into prepared muffin tin, filling cups to the top. Bake in preheated oven for 25 minutes.

Wholesome Healthy Muffins

Apple-Filled Bran Muffins

1/3 cup	chopped apple	75 mL
1/4 cup	chopped walnuts	50 mL
2 tbsp	packed brown sugar	25 mL
1 tbsp	softened butter	15 mL
1/2 tsp	cinnamon	2 mL
1 1/4 cups	all-purpose flour	300 mL
1/3 cup	granulated sugar	75 mL
1 tbsp	baking powder	15 mL
1/4 tsp	salt	1 mL
1 cup	whole bran cereal	250 mL
1 cup	milk	250 mL
1	egg, beaten	1
2 tbsp	vegetable oil	25 mL

Preheat oven to 400° F (200° C)
12-cup muffin tin, paper-lined

1. In a small bowl, combine apple, walnuts, brown sugar, butter and cinnamon. Set aside.
2. In a large bowl, combine flour, sugar, baking powder and salt.
3. In another bowl, combine cereal and milk. Let stand for 5 to 10 minutes. Stir in egg and oil. Add to flour mixture, stirring just until blended.
4. Spoon batter into prepared muffin tin, filling cups only half full. Spoon in 1 tsp (5 mL) apple filling and then top with remaining batter. Bake in pre-heated oven for 20 minutes or until golden brown.

Apple Bran Streusel Muffins

1/4 cup	all-purpose flour	50 mL
1/4 cup	packed brown sugar	50 mL
1/2 tsp	cinnamon	2 mL
2 tbsp	cold butter	25 mL
2 cups	all-purpose flour	500 mL
1 cup	natural bran	250 mL
3/4 cup	lightly packed brown sugar	175 mL
1 tbsp	baking powder	15 mL
1/2 tsp	baking soda	2 mL
1 tsp	cinnamon	5 mL
1 tsp	salt	5 mL
2	large apples, unpeeled and chopped	2
1 cup	milk	250 mL
1/2 cup	vegetable oil	125 mL
2	eggs	2

Preheat oven to 400° F (200° C)
Muffin tin, greased or paper-lined

1. In a small bowl, combine flour, 1/4 cup (50 mL) brown sugar and cinnamon. With a pastry blender, cut in butter until mixture is crumbly. Set aside.
2. In a large bowl, combine flour, bran, 3/4 cup (175 mL) brown sugar, baking powder, baking soda, cinnamon and salt. Fold in chopped apples.
3. In another bowl beat together milk, oil and eggs. Pour into apple mixture and stir just until blended.
4. Spoon batter into prepared muffin tin, filling cups three-quarters full. Sprinkle with topping and bake in preheated oven for 25 to 30 minutes.

HINT: Store brown sugar, raisins, nuts, bran, etc. in glass jars to keep fresh.

Branicot Pecan Muffins

1 cup	boiling water	250 mL
2 cups	100% bran cereal	500 mL
1/2 cup	butter *or* margarine	125 mL
1	egg	1
1/2 cup	milk	125 mL
2 tbsp	molasses	25 mL
1 1/2 cups	all-purpose flour	375 mL
1 cup	chopped dried apricots	250 mL
1 cup	chopped pecans	250 mL
1/2 cup	firmly packed brown sugar	125 mL
1 tbsp	baking powder	15 mL
1/2 tsp	salt	2 mL

Preheat oven to 400° F (200° C)
Muffin tin, greased or paper-lined

1. In a small bowl, pour boiling water over cereal and butter. Stir until butter melts and set aside to cool.

2. In another bowl, combine egg, milk and molasses. Stir in cooled cereal mixture.

3. In a large bowl, combine flour, apricots, pecans, brown sugar, baking powder and salt. Add cereal mixture, stirring just until moistened and blended.

4. Spoon batter into prepared muffin tin, filling cups to the top. Bake in preheated oven for 15 to 20 minutes or until golden brown.

HINT: For stale nuts, place in a 250° F (120° C) oven for 5 to 10 minutes. The heat will freshen them.

Double Cheese Bran Muffins

1 cup	boiling water	250 mL
1 1/2 cups	100% bran cereal	375 mL
1/4 cup	butter *or* margarine	50 mL
1/2 cup	milk	125 mL
1	egg	1
1 1/2 cups	all-purpose flour	375 mL
1/4 cup	granulated sugar	50 mL
1 tbsp	baking powder	15 mL
1/2 tsp	salt	2 mL
1 1/2 cups	shredded old Cheddar cheese	375 mL
2 tbsp	grated Parmesan cheese	25 mL

Preheat oven to 400° F (200° C)
12-cup muffin tin, greased or paper-lined

1. In a medium bowl, pour boiling water over cereal and butter. Stir until butter melts. Set aside to cool. Stir in milk and egg.

2. In a large bowl, combine flour, sugar, baking powder and salt. Stir in 1 1/4 cups (300 mL) Cheddar cheese and Parmesan cheese. Add cereal mixture, stirring just until moist and blended.

3. Spoon batter into prepared muffin tin, filling cups three-quarters full. Sprinkle with remaining Cheddar cheese. Bake in preheated oven for 20 to 25 minutes or until golden brown.

Date Bran Muffins

1 1/2 cups	natural bran	375 mL
3/4 cup	all-purpose flour *or* cake-and-pastry flour	175 mL
1 tsp	baking soda	5 mL
1 tsp	salt	5 mL
1	egg	1
1/2 cup	lightly packed brown sugar	125 mL
1 tbsp	vegetable oil	15 mL
1 cup	buttermilk *or* sour milk	250 mL
1 cup	chopped dates	250 mL
1 cup	hot water	250 mL
1/2 cup	lightly packed brown sugar	125 mL
1 tsp	lemon juice	5 mL

Preheat oven to 375° F (190° C)
Muffin tin, greased or paper-lined

1. In a large bowl, combine bran, flour, baking soda and salt.

2. In another bowl, beat together egg, brown sugar, oil and buttermilk. Pour into dry ingredients and stir just until blended.

3. In another bowl, combine dates, hot water, brown sugar and lemon juice. Add to batter, stirring just until blended.

4. Spoon batter into prepared muffin tin, filling cups three-quarters full. Bake in preheated oven for 20 to 25 minutes.

HINT: Dates, marshmallows and any sticky ingredients can be cut easily with scissors dipped in hot water.

Sunburst Bran Muffins

2 cups	all-purpose flour	500 mL
1 tbsp	baking powder	15 mL
1/2 tsp	salt	2 mL
1	egg	1
1 1/4 cups	milk	300 mL
1 1/2 cups	100% bran cereal	375 mL
1/3 cup	margarine, melted	75 mL
1/2 cup	raisins (optional)	125 mL
1/2 cup	firmly packed brown sugar	125 mL
1 tsp	grated orange zest	5 mL
1/2 cup	orange juice	125 mL

Preheat oven to 400° F (200° C)
Muffin tin, greased or paper-lined

1. In a large bowl, combine flour, baking powder and salt. Make a well in the center.

2. In another bowl beat egg with a fork. Stir in milk, cereal, margarine, raisins (if using), sugar, zest and juice. Mix well. Add to flour mixture, stirring just until blended and moistened.

3. Spoon batter into prepared muffin tin, filling cups to the top. Bake in preheated oven for about 20 minutes.

Cheddar Bacon Muffins

2 cups	all-purpose flour	500 mL
2 tbsp	granulated sugar	25 mL
1 tbsp	baking powder	15 mL
1/4 tsp	salt	1 mL
1/2 cup	grated Cheddar cheese	125 mL
4 or 5	slices bacon, cooked crisp and crumbled	4 or 5
1	egg, slightly beaten	1
1 cup	milk	250 mL
1/4 cup	vegetable oil	50 mL

Preheat oven to 400° F (200° C)
Muffin tin, greased or paper-lined

1. In a large bowl, combine flour, sugar, baking powder, salt, cheese and bacon. Blend well and make a well in the center.

2. In another bowl, whisk together egg, milk and oil. Pour into dry ingredients and stir just until moist and lumpy.

3. Spoon batter into prepared muffin tin, filling cups to the top. Bake in preheated oven for 20 to 25 minutes.

VARIATIONS

Increase grated Cheddar cheese to 1 cup (250 mL). Use the added 1/2 cup (125 mL) to sprinkle over tops before baking.

Replace milk with 1 can (10 oz [284 mL]) of any cream soup such as mushroom or chicken.

Omit the bacon and substitute 2/3 cup (150 mL) chopped cooked ham. Substitute Swiss cheese for Cheddar and increase oil to 1/3 cup (75 mL).

Bran n' Cheese Muffins

1 cup	All-Bran cereal	250 mL
1 1/4 cups	buttermilk *or* sour milk	300 mL
1	egg	1
1/4 cup	vegetable oil	50 mL
1 1/2 cups	all-purpose flour	375 mL
1/4 cup	granulated sugar	50 mL
1 1/2 tsp	baking powder	7 mL
1/2 tsp	baking soda	2 mL
1/2 tsp	salt	2 mL
1 cup	grated sharp Cheddar cheese	250 mL

Preheat oven to 400° F (200° C)
Two 8-cup muffin tins, greased or paper-lined

1. In a small bowl, combine cereal and buttermilk. Let stand 5 minutes.

2. In another bowl beat egg. Add oil and cereal mixture.

3. In a large bowl, combine flour, sugar, baking powder, baking soda, salt and cheese. Add egg mixture, stirring just until moistened and lumpy.

4. Spoon batter into prepared muffin tins, filling cups three-quarters full. Bake in preheated oven for 20 to 25 minutes.

HINT: To prevent a block of cheese from becoming moldy, wrap a cloth saturated in white vinegar around the cheese.

Cheddar Cheese Muffins with Apple Butter

2 cups	all-purpose flour	500 mL
1/2 cup	granulated sugar	125 mL
1 tbsp	baking powder	15 mL
1/2 tsp	salt	2 mL
1/2 tsp	baking soda	2 mL
2 cups	grated Cheddar cheese	500 mL
1 cup	plain yogurt	250 mL
1/4 cup	butter or margarine, melted	50 mL
2	eggs, beaten	2
APPLE BUTTER		
1/2 cup	softened butter	125 mL
1/2 cup	apple jelly	125 mL
1/4 tsp	cinnamon	1 mL

Preheat oven to 400° F (200° C)
Muffin tin, greased or paper-lined

1. In a large bowl, combine flour, sugar, baking powder, salt and baking soda. Stir in cheese, mixing well. Make a well in the center.

2. In another bowl, whisk together yogurt, butter and eggs. Add quickly to dry ingredients, stirring just until blended and lumpy.

3. Spoon batter into prepared muffin tin, filling to the top. Bake in preheated oven for 18 to 20 minutes or until golden brown.

4. Meanwhile, prepare Apple Butter. In a bowl beat butter until creamy. Add jelly and cinnamon, blending well. Serve with warm muffins.

Cheddar Brunch Muffins

2 cups	all-purpose flour	500 mL
2 tbsp	granulated sugar	25 mL
2 1/2 tsp	baking powder	12 mL
1/2 tsp	salt	2 mL
1 1/2 cups	shredded Cheddar cheese	375 mL
1	egg	1
1 cup	milk	250 mL
1/4 cup	melted butter	50 mL

Preheat oven to 400° F (200° C)
Muffin tin, greased or paper-lined

1. In a large bowl, sift together flour, sugar, baking powder and salt. Fold in cheese, making sure to coat well with flour. Add unbeaten egg, milk and butter, stirring quickly just until blended. Do not overmix.

2. Spoon batter into prepared muffin tin, filling cups three-quarters full. Bake in preheated oven for 20 to 30 minutes.

HINT: A dull knife works much better than a sharp one for slicing cheese.

Cottage Marmalade Muffins

1/2 cup + 1 tbsp	all-purpose flour	125 mL + 15 mL
1 tsp	baking powder	5 mL
1/8 tsp	salt	0.5 mL
1	egg, lightly beaten	1
2/3 cup	small-curd cottage cheese	150 mL
1 tbsp	vegetable oil	15 mL
1 tsp	honey	5 mL
2 tbsp	orange marmalade	25 mL

Preheat oven to 400° F (200° C)
6-cup muffin tin, greased or paper-lined

1. In a large bowl, sift together flour, baking powder and salt. Make a well in the center.

2. In another bowl, whisk together egg, cheese, oil and honey. Add to dry ingredients, stirring just until moistened.

3. Spoon batter into prepared muffin tin, filling cups half full. Add 1 tsp (5 mL) marmalade to each cup and top with remaining batter. Bake in preheated oven for 15 to 20 minutes.

Cheesy Lemony Muffins

1 1/2 cups	all-purpose flour	375 mL
1/4 cup	granulated sugar	50 mL
1 1/2 tsp	baking powder	7 mL
1/2 tsp	baking soda	2 mL
1/2 tsp	salt	2 mL
1	small lemon	1
1 cup	creamed cottage cheese	250 mL
1 cup	All-Bran cereal	250 mL
2 tbsp	milk	25 mL
2	eggs	2
1/4 cup	butter or margarine, melted	50 mL
1/4 cup	liquid honey	50 mL

Preheat oven to 400° F (200° C)
12-cup muffin tin, greased or paper-lined

1. In a large bowl, combine flour, sugar, baking powder, baking soda and salt. Make a well in the center.

2. Peel lemon very thinly to remove zest. Then remove white pith, seeds and inner membranes from the rest of the lemon. Put zest and pulp into a food processor or blender and process until smooth. Add cottage cheese and process again. Stir in cereal and milk. Let stand for 5 minutes.

3. Stir in eggs, margarine and honey. Pour into flour mixture, stirring just until moistened and lumpy.

4. Spoon batter into prepared muffin tin, filling cups to the top. Bake in preheated oven for 20 minutes or until golden brown and firm to the touch.

Easy Oat Bran Muffins

1 1/4 cups	all-purpose flour	300 mL
1/2 cup	packed brown sugar	125 mL
3/4 cup	oat bran	175 mL
1/4 cup	granulated sugar	50 mL
2 tsp	baking powder	10 mL
1/2 tsp	salt	2 mL
1/4 tsp	cinnamon	1 mL
1	egg, slightly beaten	1
1 cup	milk	250 mL
1/4 cup	vegetable oil	50 mL
1/4 cup	liquid honey	50 mL

Preheat oven to 400° F (200° C)
Muffin tin, greased or paper-lined

1. In a large bowl, mix together flour, brown sugar, oat bran, sugar, baking powder, salt and cinnamon. Make a well in the center. Add egg, milk, oil and honey. Mix just until moist and blended.

2. Spoon batter into prepared muffin tin, filling cups three-quarters full. Bake in preheated oven for 20 to 25 minutes.

Oldtime Classic Oat Bran Muffins

1 1/2 cups	oat bran	375 mL
1 cup	buttermilk	250 mL
1	egg	1
1/3 cup	vegetable oil	75 mL
1/2 cup	packed brown sugar	125 mL
1/2 tsp	vanilla	2 mL
1 cup	all-purpose flour	250 mL
1 tsp	baking powder	5 mL
1 tsp	baking soda	5 mL
1/2 tsp	salt	2 mL
1/2 tsp	cinnamon	2 mL
1/2 cup	raisins	125 mL

Preheat oven to 375° F (190° C)
12-cup muffin tin, greased or paper-lined

1. In a large bowl, combine oat bran and buttermilk. Let stand.

2. In another bowl, beat egg lightly. Add oil, sugar and vanilla. Stir into bran mixture.

3. In another bowl, sift together flour, baking powder, baking soda, salt and cinnamon. Stir into bran mixture just until moistened. Fold in raisins.

4. Spoon batter into prepared muffin tin, filling cups three-quarters full. Bake in preheated oven for 15 to 20 minutes or until firm to the touch.

Applesauce Oat Bran Muffins

1 cup	oat bran	250 mL
1 cup	all-purpose flour	250 mL
1/4 cup	granulated sugar	50 mL
1 tbsp	baking powder	15 mL
1/2 tsp	salt	2 mL
1/4 cup	raisins	50 mL
2	eggs	2
1 cup	unsweetened applesauce	250 mL
3 tbsp	milk	45 mL
3 tbsp	vegetable oil	45 mL
TOPPING		
1 tbsp	granulated sugar	15 mL
1/2 tsp	cinnamon	2 mL
1/4 cup	chopped walnuts	50 mL

Preheat oven to 425° F (220° C)
12-cup muffin tin, greased or foil-lined

1. In a large bowl, combine oat bran, flour, sugar, baking powder, salt and raisins.

2. In another bowl, beat eggs lightly with a fork. Stir in applesauce, milk and oil. Pour into dry ingredients. Stir just until moist and blended.

3. Spoon batter into prepared muffin tin, filling cups three-quarters full. Sprinkle with sugar, cinnamon and walnuts. Bake in preheated oven for 20 minutes.

HINT: Here's a great way to crush nuts and avoid messy clean-ups: Place nuts in a plastic bag or between sheets of wax paper and crush with a rolling pin.

Apple Walnut Oat Bran Muffins

1 cup	all-purpose flour	250 mL
1 cup	whole-wheat flour	250 mL
1 cup	oat bran	250 mL
1 tbsp	baking powder	15 mL
1 1/2 tsp	baking soda	7 mL
1 tsp	cinnamon	5 mL
1 cup	chopped walnuts	250 mL
1 cup	grated unpeeled apple	250 mL
1/2 cup	packed brown sugar	125 mL
1 1/2 cups	buttermilk	375 mL
3	egg whites	3
5 tbsp	vegetable oil	75 mL

Preheat oven to 400° F (200° C)
Muffin tin, greased or paper-lined

1. In a large bowl, combine all-purpose flour, whole-wheat flour, oat bran, baking powder, baking soda, cinnamon, walnuts and apple.

2. In another bowl, dissolve brown sugar in buttermilk. Add egg whites and oil, beating lightly with a fork until well blended. Add to dry ingredients, stirring just until moistened. Do not overmix.

3. Spoon batter into prepared muffin tin, filling cups to the top. Bake in preheated oven for 20 minutes.

Banana Oat Bran Muffins

1 1/4 cups	all-purpose flour	300 mL
3/4 cup	oat bran	175 mL
1 tsp	baking powder	5 mL
1 tsp	baking soda	5 mL
1/4 tsp	salt	1 mL
1	egg	1
1/3 cup	vegetable oil	75 mL
1/3 cup	lightly packed brown sugar	75 mL
1 cup	mashed banana	250 mL
1/2 cup	buttermilk *or* sour milk	125 mL
2 tbsp	molasses	25 mL
3/4 cup	raisins	175 mL

Preheat oven to 375° F (190° C)
12-cup muffin tin, greased or paper-lined

1. In a large bowl, combine flour, oat bran, baking powder, baking soda and salt.

2. In another bowl, whisk together egg, oil, brown sugar, banana, buttermilk, molasses and raisins. Add to dry ingredients, stirring just until blended and lumpy.

3. Spoon batter into prepared muffin tin, filling cups three-quarters full. Bake in preheated oven for 20 to 25 minutes.

Berry Oat Bran Muffins

1	egg, slightly beaten	1
1/2 cup	milk *or* yogurt	125 mL
1/4 cup	vegetable oil	50 mL
1/4 cup	honey	50 mL
2/3 cup	applesauce	150 mL
1 tsp	vanilla	5 mL
1 cup	whole-wheat flour	250 mL
1 tsp	baking powder	5 mL
1 tsp	baking soda	5 mL
1 cup	oat bran	250 mL
1 cup	berries (saskatoon or any other)	250 mL

Preheat oven to 375° F (190° C)
Muffin tin, greased or paper-lined

1. In a blender or food processor, combine egg, milk, oil, honey, applesauce and vanilla. Mix well and transfer to a large bowl.

2. In another bowl, combine flour, baking powder, baking soda, oat bran and berries. Stir into egg mixture just until blended. Do not overmix.

3. Spoon batter into prepared muffin tin. Bake in preheated oven for about 15 minutes.

Buttermilk Oat Bran Muffins

1 cup	all-purpose flour	250 mL
1 cup	oat bran	250 mL
1/3 cup	granulated sugar	75 mL
1 tsp	baking powder	5 mL
1 tsp	baking soda	5 mL
1/2 tsp	cinnamon	2 mL
1/4 tsp	salt	1 mL
1	egg	1
3/4 cup	buttermilk	175 mL
1/4 cup	corn oil	50 mL
1 tbsp	grated orange zest	15 mL
2 tbsp	orange juice	25 mL
1 cup	raisins *or* chopped dates	250 mL

Preheat oven to 400° F (200° C)
12-cup muffin tin, greased

1. In a large bowl, combine flour, oat bran, sugar, baking powder, baking soda, cinnamon and salt. Mix well and make a well in the center.

2. In another bowl, whisk together egg, buttermilk, oil, zest and juice. Pour into dry ingredients and stir just until moist and blended. Fold in raisins.

3. Spoon batter into prepared muffin tin, dividing evenly. Bake in preheated oven for 20 to 25 minutes or until top springs back when lightly touched.

HINT: If you have leftover raisins and nuts, chop them together for a great snack and healthy treat.

Carrot Pecan Oat Bran Muffins

1 cup	all-purpose flour	250 mL
1 cup	oat bran	250 mL
2 tsp	baking soda	10 mL
1 tsp	baking powder	5 mL
1/2 tsp	salt	2 mL
2 tsp	cinnamon	10 mL
1 cup	packed brown sugar	250 mL
1 1/2 cups	shredded carrots	375 mL
2	large apples, shredded	2
1/2 cup	raisins	125 mL
1 cup	chopped pecans	250 mL
1/4 cup	vegetable oil	50 mL
1/2 cup	skim milk	125 mL
2	eggs, lightly beaten	2
1 tsp	vanilla	5 mL

Preheat oven to 375° F (190° C)
18-cup muffin tin, greased

1. In a large bowl, combine flour, oat bran, baking soda, baking powder, salt and cinnamon. Add sugar and mix well. Stir in carrots, apples, raisins and pecans. Make a well in the center. Add oil, milk, eggs and vanilla, stirring just until moist and blended.

2. Spoon batter evenly into prepared muffin tin. Bake in preheated oven for about 20 minutes.

Honey Date Oat Bran Muffins

2 cups	oat and wheat cereal (such as Kellogg's Common Sense)	500 mL
1 1/4 cups	skim milk	300 mL
1/4 cup	liquid honey	50 mL
2	egg whites	2
3 tbsp	vegetable oil	45 mL
3/4 cup	chopped pitted dates	175 mL
1 1/4 cups	all-purpose flour	300 mL
1 tbsp	baking powder	15 mL
1/4 tsp	salt	1 mL
3/4 tsp	cinnamon	4 mL
1/4 tsp	nutmeg	1 mL

Preheat oven to 400° F (200° C)
12-cup muffin tin, greased

1. In a large bowl, combine cereal, milk, honey, egg whites, oil and dates.

2. In another bowl, combine flour, baking powder, salt, cinnamon and nutmeg. Add to cereal mixture, stirring just until well blended. Batter will be lumpy.

3. Spoon batter into prepared muffin tin. Bake in preheated oven for 15 to 20 minutes or until golden brown.

Lemon Banana Oat Bran Muffins

1 1/2 cups	all-purpose flour	375 mL
3/4 cup	Oat Bran cereal	175 mL
1 tsp	baking soda	5 mL
1/2 tsp	salt	2 mL
1 cup	granulated sugar	250 mL
1/2 cup	margarine *or* butter	125 mL
1 cup	mashed ripe bananas	250 mL
2	eggs	2
1/2 tsp	grated lemon zest	2 mL
1/3 cup	milk	75 mL
1 tsp	lemon juice	5 mL
1/2 cup	chopped nuts	125 mL

Preheat oven to 400° F (200° C)
Muffin tin, greased or paper-lined

1. In a bowl combine flour, cereal, baking soda and salt. Mix together well.

2. In a large bowl, cream together sugar and margarine until light and fluffy. Stir in bananas, eggs and zest.

3. In another bowl, combine milk and juice. Add to banana mixture alternately with flour mixture, stirring after each addition. Fold in nuts.

4. Spoon batter into prepared muffin tin, filling cups to the top. Bake in preheated oven for 15 to 20 minutes.

Oat Bran Raisin Muffins

2 cups	oat bran	500 mL
1/4 cup	packed brown sugar	50 mL
2 tsp	baking powder	10 mL
1/2 cup	raisins	125 mL
1 cup	plain yogurt	250 mL
2	egg whites, slightly beaten	2
1/4 cup	milk	50 mL
1/4 cup	honey *or* molasses	50 mL
2 tbsp	vegetable oil	25 mL
1 tsp	grated orange zest	5 mL

Preheat oven to 400° F (200° C)
12-cup muffin tin, greased or paper-lined

1. In a large bowl, combine oat bran, sugar, baking powder and raisins. Make a well in the center. Add yogurt, egg whites, milk, honey, oil and zest, stirring just until blended.

2. Spoon batter into prepared muffin tin. Bake in preheated oven for 20 minutes.

Quick Oatmeal Muffins

1 cup	all-purpose flour	250 mL
1/4 cup	granulated sugar	50 mL
3 tsp	baking powder	15 mL
1/2 tsp	salt	2 mL
1 cup	quick-cooking oats	250 mL
1	egg, slightly beaten	1
1 cup	milk	250 mL
3 tbsp	vegetable oil	45 mL

Preheat oven to 425° F (220° C)
Muffin tin, greased or paper-lined

1. In a large bowl, combine flour, sugar, baking powder, salt, oats, egg, milk and oil. Stir just until moist and blended.

2. Spoon batter into prepared muffin tin, filling cups three-quarters full. Bake in preheated oven for about 15 minutes.

HINT: Olive oil will stay fresh longer if you add a cube of sugar to the bottle.

Apple Date Oatmeal Muffins

2/3 cup + 2 tbsp	quick oats	150 mL + 25 mL
1 tsp	firmly packed light brown sugar	5 mL
1/4 tsp	cinnamon	1 mL
1 cup less 1 tbsp	all-purpose flour	250 mL less 15 mL
2 tbsp	granulated sugar	25 mL
2 tsp	baking powder	10 mL
1 tbsp	grated orange zest	15 mL
1/2 cup	orange juice	125 mL
1	egg	1
1/4 cup	margarine, melted	50 mL
1	small apple, cored and chopped	1
8	dates, pitted and chopped	8

Preheat oven to 400° F (200° C)
8-cup muffin tin, paper-lined

1. In a small skillet over medium heat, cook 1/3 cup (75 mL) oats, stirring often, for 3 to 4 minutes or until golden. Remove from heat and stir in brown sugar and cinnamon. Set aside for topping.

2. In a large bowl, combine remaining oats, flour, sugar and baking powder. Make a well in the center.

3. In another bowl, combine zest, juice, egg and margarine. Add to the flour mixture, stirring just until moistened. Fold in apple and dates.

4. Spoon batter into prepared muffin tin, filling cups two-thirds full. Sprinkle with topping. Bake in preheated oven for 20 to 25 minutes.

Apricot Oatmeal Muffins

3/4 cup	boiling water	175 mL
1 cup	quick-cooking oats	250 mL
1/2 cup	chopped dried apricots	125 mL
1/2 cup	margarine *or* butter	125 mL
1	egg	1
1 cup	milk	250 mL
2 1/2 cups	all-purpose flour	625 mL
1/2 cup	firmly packed brown sugar	125 mL
1 tbsp	baking powder	15 mL
1/2 tsp	salt	2 mL

Preheat oven to 400° F (200° C)
Muffin tin, greased or paper-lined

1. In a medium bowl, pour boiling water over oats, apricots and margarine. Stir until margarine melts. Set aside to cool. Add egg and milk.

2. In a large bowl, combine flour, brown sugar, baking powder and salt. Add oat mixture, stirring just until blended and moistened. Do not overmix.

3. Spoon batter into prepared muffin tin, filling cups to the top. Bake in preheated oven for about 20 minutes.

Cranberry Oatmeal Muffins

1/2 cup	finely chopped walnuts	125 mL
1/2 cup	dried cranberries	125 mL
1 1/2 cups	all-purpose flour	375 mL
1 tbsp	baking powder	15 mL
3/4 tsp	salt	4 mL
3/4 cup	old-fashioned oats	175 mL
3 tbsp	softened butter or margarine	45 mL
3/4 cup	firmly packed light brown sugar	175 mL
3/4 cup	milk	175 mL
1	egg	1

Preheat oven to 350° F (180° C)
Muffin tin, greased

1. In a small bowl, toss together nuts, cranberries and 1 tsp (5 mL) flour. Set aside.

2. In a large bowl, combine remaining flour, baking powder and salt. Stir in oats.

3. In another bowl, whisk together butter, sugar, milk and egg, blending well. Add to flour mixture, stirring just until evenly moist and blended. Fold in nut mixture.

4. Spoon batter into prepared muffin tin, filling cups to the top. Bake in preheated oven for about 20 minutes.

Oatmeal Date Muffins

1 cup	all-purpose flour	250 mL
2 tsp	baking powder	10 mL
1/2 tsp	baking soda	2 mL
1/2 tsp	salt	2 mL
1 cup	old-fashioned rolled oats	250 mL
1 cup	buttermilk	250 mL
1/2 cup	packed dark brown sugar	125 mL
1	egg, beaten	1
1/2 cup	butter or margarine, melted	125 mL
1/2 cup	chopped moist dates	125 mL

Preheat oven to 375° F (190° C)
12-cup muffin tin, greased or paper-lined

1. In a medium bowl, sift together flour, baking powder, baking soda and salt.

2. In a large bowl, combine oats and buttermilk. Let stand for 5 minutes. Add sugar, egg and butter, mixing well. Fold in dates. Add to flour mixture, stirring just until moist and blended.

3. Spoon batter into prepared muffin tin, filling cups three-quarters full. Bake in preheated oven for 25 to 30 minutes.

Fruity Oatmeal Muffins

1 cup	all-purpose flour	250 mL
1 tsp	baking powder	5 mL
1/4 tsp	pumpkin pie spice	1 mL
1 cup	packaged dried fruit	250 mL
1/2 cup	softened butter or margarine	125 mL
2/3 cup	granulated sugar	150 mL
6	eggs	6
1 tsp	vanilla	5 mL
1/3 cup	rolled oats	75 mL

Preheat oven to 350° F (180° C)
12-cup muffin tin, greased or paper-lined

1. In a small bowl, combine flour, baking powder and pumpkin pie spice. Take 1 tbsp (15 mL) of this flour mixture and toss in another bowl, with dried fruit.

2. In a large bowl, beat butter and sugar on medium speed until light and fluffy. Beat in eggs and blend well. Reduce speed to low and add vanilla. Gradually add flour mixture, beating just until blended. Stir in fruit mixture and oats.

3. Spoon batter into prepared muffin tin, filling cups three-quarters full. Bake in preheated oven for 20 minutes or until golden brown.

Whole-Wheat Honey Oatmeal Muffins

1 cup	whole-wheat flour	250 mL
1 cup	rolled oats	250 mL
1 1/2 tsp	baking powder	7 mL
1 tsp	baking soda	5 mL
1/2 tsp	salt	2 mL
1/4 tsp	cinnamon	1 mL
1/4 cup	packed brown sugar	50 mL
1	egg	1
1/4 cup	butter or margarine, melted and cooled	50 mL
1/4 cup	honey	50 mL
1 1/4 cups	buttermilk	300 mL

Preheat oven to 400° F (200° C)
Muffin tin, greased or paper-lined

1. In a large bowl, combine flour, oats, baking powder, baking soda, salt, cinnamon and brown sugar.

2. In another bowl, whisk together egg, butter, honey and buttermilk. Pour into flour mixture, stirring just until moistened and blended.

3. Spoon batter into prepared muffin tin, filling cups to the top. Bake in preheated oven for 15 minutes.

HINT: Use a muffin pan for a manicure tray. Put bottles of base, topcoat, various colors nail polish , cotton, etc. into each cup.

BERRY OAT BRAN MUFFINS (PAGE 122) ➤

Lemon-Glazed Apple Oatmeal Muffins

1 1/4 cups	all-purpose flour	300 mL
1/2 cup	packed light brown sugar	125 mL
1 1/2 tsp	baking powder	7 mL
1 tsp	baking soda	5 mL
1 tsp	cinnamon	5 mL
1/2 tsp	salt	2 mL
1/4 tsp	ground nutmeg	1 mL
1	egg	1
1/2 cup	milk	125 mL
1/4 cup	vegetable oil	50 mL
2 tbsp	lemon juice	25 mL
3/4 cup	quick-cooking oats	175 mL
1 cup	finely chopped apples	250 mL
1/2 cup	chopped nuts	125 mL

LEMON GLAZE

1/2 cup	icing sugar	125 mL
1 tbsp	lemon juice	15 mL
1 tbsp	butter or margarine, melted	15 mL

Preheat oven to 400° F (200° C)
Muffin tin, greased or paper-lined

1. In a medium bowl, combine flour, sugar, baking powder, baking soda, cinnamon, salt and nutmeg.

2. In a large bowl, beat egg. Add milk, oil and lemon juice. Stir in oats and mix well. Add flour mixture, blending well. Add apples and nuts, stirring just until moistened and lumpy. Do not overmix.

3. Spoon batter into prepared muffin tin, filling cups three-quarters full. Bake in preheated oven for 20 minutes or until golden brown.

4. Meanwhile, in a small bowl, combine icing sugar, juice and butter. Remove muffins from tin and place on a plate. Drizzle with lemon glaze.

HINT: If you reduce or eliminate salt in recipes, use more herbs and spices to enhance the flavor. Experiment with small amounts at first, such as 1/4 tsp (1 mL).

◄ PEACHY OATMEAL MUFFINS (PAGE 130)

Orange Date Oatmeal Muffins

1 1/4 cups	milk	300 mL
1 cup	quick-cooking oats	250 mL
1	medium orange, cut into quarters and seeded	1
1	egg	1
3/4 cup	firmly packed brown sugar	175 mL
1/2 cup	butter or margarine, melted	125 mL
1/2 cup	chopped dates	125 mL
2 cups	all-purpose flour	500 mL
1 tbsp	baking powder	15 mL
1/2 tsp	salt	2 mL

Preheat oven to 400° F (200° C)
12-cup muffin tin, greased or paper-lined

1. In a bowl pour milk over oats. Let stand for 5 minutes.

2. In a food processor or blender, process orange until finely chopped. Stir into oat mixture. Add egg, sugar, butter and dates.

3. In a large bowl, combine flour, baking powder and salt. Add oat mixture, stirring just until blended. Do not overmix.

4. Spoon batter into prepared muffin tin, dividing evenly. Bake in preheated oven for 20 to 25 minutes or until golden brown.

Peachy Oatmeal Muffins

2 cups	whole-wheat flour	500 mL
1 cup	rolled oats	250 mL
1/2 cup	unprocessed wheat bran	125 mL
1/2 cup	packed brown sugar	125 mL
1 1/2 tsp	baking soda	7 mL
1 tsp	salt	5 mL
2	eggs	2
1 1/2 cups	buttermilk	375 mL
1/4 cup	vegetable oil	50 mL
3 tsp	orange zest	15 mL
1 1/2 tsp	cinnamon	7 mL
3	fresh peaches, finely chopped	3

Preheat oven to 400° F (200° C)
Muffin tin, paper-lined

1. In a large bowl, combine flour, oats, wheat bran, sugar, baking soda and salt. Make a well in the center.

2. In another bowl, whisk together eggs, buttermilk and oil. Stir in zest and cinnamon. Add to dry ingredients, stirring just until moistened. Fold in peaches.

3. Spoon batter into prepared muffin tin, filling cups three-quarters full. Bake in preheated oven for about 20 minutes.

VARIATIONS

 You could replace peaches with 2 cups (500 mL) fresh chopped pears, plums or nectarines.

Oatmeal Raisin Breakfast Muffins

1/2 cup	raisins	125 mL
1/4 cup	all-purpose flour	50 mL
1/4 cup	butter *or* margarine	50 mL
1/3 cup	granulated sugar	75 mL
2	eggs	2
2/3 cup	milk	150 mL
3/4 cup	all-purpose flour	175 mL
3 tsp	baking powder	15 mL
3/4 tsp	salt	4 mL
1 cup	rolled oats	250 mL

Preheat oven to 400° F (200° C)
12-cup muffin tin, greased

1. In a small bowl, toss together raisins and 1/4 cup (50 mL) flour. Set aside.

2. In a large bowl, cream together butter and sugar. Add eggs one at a time, beating after each addition. Add milk.

3. In another bowl, combine 3/4 cup (175 mL) flour, baking powder and salt. Pour into wet ingredients. Add oats, stirring just until blended. Fold in dredged raisins.

4. Spoon batter into prepared muffin tin, dividing evenly. Bake in preheated oven for 20 to 25 minutes.

HINT: In baking only, you can use 1 cup (250 mL) shortening plus 1/2 tsp (2 mL) salt to replace 1 cup (250 mL) butter.

Favorite Wheat Germ Muffins

1 cup	all-purpose flour	250 mL
1 cup	toasted wheat germ	250 mL
4 tsp	baking powder	20 mL
1/4 tsp	baking soda	1 mL
1/2 tsp	salt	2 mL
1	egg	1
2 tbsp	softened butter or margarine	25 mL
1/4 cup	packed brown sugar	50 mL
	Grated zest of 1 orange	
1/4 cup	orange juice	50 mL
3/4 cup	plain yogurt	175 mL

Preheat oven to 425° F (200° C)
Muffin tin, greased or paper-lined

1. In a large bowl, combine flour, wheat germ, baking powder, baking soda and salt. Make a well in the center.

2. In another bowl, cream together egg, butter and sugar. Stir in zest and orange juice, mixing well. Add yogurt. Add to dry ingredients, stirring just until blended. Do not overmix.

3. Spoon batter into prepared muffin tin, filling cups to the top. Bake in preheated oven for about 15 minutes.

Apple Streusel Wheat Germ Muffins

1/4 cup	granulated sugar	50 mL
1/2 tsp	cinnamon	2 mL
1/3 cup	chopped nuts	75 mL
2 tbsp	butter or margarine, melted	25 mL

1 1/2 cups	all-purpose flour	375 mL
1/2 cup	wheat germ	125 mL
1/4 cup	granulated sugar	50 mL
1 tbsp	baking powder	15 mL
3/4 tsp	cinnamon	4 mL
1/2 tsp	salt	2 mL
1 cup	chopped peeled apple	250 mL
1	egg	1
1 cup	milk	250 mL
1/4 cup	vegetable oil	50 mL

Preheat oven to 400° F (200° C)
Muffin tin, greased or paper-lined

1. In a bowl combine sugar, cinnamon, nuts and butter. Set aside.

2. In a large bowl, combine flour, wheat germ, sugar, baking powder, cinnamon and salt. Stir in apple.

3. In another bowl, whisk together egg, milk and oil. Add to dry ingredients, stirring just until moistened.

4. Spoon batter into prepared muffin tin, filling cups two-thirds full. Sprinkle with topping. Bake in preheated oven for 20 to 25 minutes or until browned.

Blueberry Wheat Germ Muffins

1 3/4 cups	all-purpose flour	425 mL
1/3 cup	wheat germ	75 mL
1/3 cup	granulated sugar	75 mL
1 tbsp	baking powder	15 mL
1 1/2 tsp	grated lemon zest	7 mL
1/2 tsp	salt	2 mL
1	egg	1
1 cup	milk	250 mL
1/4 cup	vegetable oil	50 mL
1 cup	fresh blueberries or frozen blueberries, drained	250 mL

Preheat oven to 400° F (200° C)
Muffin tin, greased or paper-lined

1. In a large bowl, combine flour, wheat germ, sugar, baking powder, zest and salt. Make a well in the center.

2. In another bowl, whisk together egg, milk and oil. Add to dry ingredients, stirring just until moist and blended. Fold in berries.

3. Spoon batter into prepared muffin tin, filling cups three-quarters full. Bake in preheated oven for 20 to 25 minutes.

Orange Wheat Germ Muffins

1 cup	all-purpose flour	250 mL
3/4 cup	wheat germ	175 mL
1/2 cup	wheat bran	125 mL
3 tsp	baking powder	15 mL
1/2 tsp	salt	2 mL
1/2 cup	brown sugar	125 mL
1/2 cup	raisins	125 mL
1	egg	1
1 cup	milk	250 mL
1/4 cup	vegetable oil	50 mL
2 tsp	grated orange zest	10 mL

Preheat oven to 400° F (200° C)
Muffin tin, greased or paper-lined

1. In a large bowl, combine flour, wheat germ, bran, baking powder, salt, sugar and raisins.

2. In another bowl, whisk together egg, milk, oil and zest. Add to dry ingredients, stirring just until moist and blended.

3. Spoon batter into prepared muffin tin, dividing evenly. Bake in preheated oven for 15 to 20 minutes or until tests done.

HINT: For plumper raisins, soak in orange juice and store in the refrigerator.

Wheat Muffins

1 cup	all-purpose flour	250 mL
1 cup	unsifted whole-wheat flour	250 mL
2 tsp	baking powder	10 mL
1 tsp	salt	5 mL
1	egg, slightly beaten	1
1/4 cup	molasses	50 mL
1 cup	milk	250 mL
1/4 cup	butter or margarine, melted	50 mL

Preheat oven to 400° F (200° C)
Muffin tin, greased or paper-lined

1. In a large bowl, combine all-purpose flour, whole-wheat flour, baking powder and salt. Make a well in the center.

2. In another bowl, combine egg, molasses, milk and butter. Add to flour mixture, stirring just until blended. Do not overmix.

3. Spoon batter into prepared muffin tin, filling cups three-quarters full. Bake in preheated oven for 25 minutes or until golden brown.

Apple Whole-Wheat Muffins

1 1/2 cups	whole-wheat flour	375 mL
1/2 cup	all-purpose flour	125 mL
2 1/2 tsp	baking powder	12 mL
3/4 tsp	salt	4 mL
1	egg, beaten	1
3/4 cup	milk	175 mL
1/3 cup	vegetable oil	75 mL
1/3 cup	honey	75 mL
1 cup	chopped apples	250 mL

Preheat oven to 400° F (200° C)
Muffin tin, greased or paper-lined

1. In a large bowl combine whole-wheat flour, all-purpose flour, baking powder and salt.
2. In another bowl, whisk together egg, milk, oil and honey. Add to flour mixture, stirring just until moist and blended. Do not overmix. Fold in apples.
3. Spoon batter into prepared muffin tin, filling cups three-quarters full. Bake in preheated oven for 18 to 20 minutes or until a toothpick inserted in center comes out clean and dry.

Whole-Wheat Date Muffins

1 cup	chopped pitted dates	250 mL
1 tsp	baking soda	5 mL
3/4 cup	boiling water	175 mL
1	egg	1
1/2 cup	granulated sugar	125 mL
1 tsp	salt	5 mL
1 tsp	vanilla	5 mL
1 1/2 cups	whole-wheat flour	375 mL
1 tsp	baking powder	5 mL
1/2 cup	chopped walnuts	125 mL
1/4 cup	butter, melted	50 mL

Preheat oven to 375° F (190° C)
Muffin tin, greased or paper-lined

1. In a large bowl, toss together dates and baking soda. Pour boiling water over top. Mix well and set aside to cool.
2. In another bowl, whisk together egg, sugar, salt and vanilla. Add to date mixture. Stir in flour, baking powder and walnuts. Add melted butter, stirring just until blended.
3. Spoon batter into prepared muffin tin, filling cups three-quarters full. Bake in preheated oven for 15 to 20 minutes.

HINT: Store shelled nuts (and coconut) in tightly covered containers in the fridge or freezer to prevent from becoming rancid. When ready to use, heat thoroughly at 350° F (180° C.)

Herbed Whole-Wheat Muffins

1 cup	whole-wheat flour	250 mL
1 cup	all-purpose flour	250 mL
1/3 cup	granulated sugar	75 mL
2 tsp	baking powder	10 mL
1/2 tsp	baking soda	2 mL
1/2 tsp	salt	2 mL
1/2 tsp	dried basil leaves	2 mL
1/4 tsp	dried marjoram leaves	1 mL
1/4 tsp	dried oregano leaves	1 mL
1/8 tsp	dried thyme leaves	.5 mL
3/4 cup	raisins	175 mL
1 cup	buttermilk	250 mL
2 tbsp	butter or margarine, melted	25 mL
1	egg, beaten	1
2 tbsp	wheat germ	25 mL

Preheat oven to 400° F (200° C)
Muffin tin, greased or paper-lined

1. In a large bowl, combine whole-wheat flour, all-purpose flour, sugar, baking powder, baking soda, salt, basil, marjoram, oregano, thyme and raisins.

2. In another bowl, whisk together buttermilk, butter and egg. Add to flour mixture, stirring just until moistened and blended.

3. Spoon batter into prepared muffin tin, filling cups two-thirds full. Sprinkle with wheat germ. Bake in preheated oven for 15 to 20 minutes or until browned.

Honey Whole-Wheat Muffins

1 cup	whole-wheat flour	250 mL
1 cup	all-purpose flour	250 mL
3 tsp	baking powder	15 mL
1 tsp	salt	5 mL
1	egg	1
1 cup	milk	250 mL
1/4 cup	vegetable oil	50 mL
1/4 cup	honey	50 mL

Preheat oven to 400° F (200° C)
12-cup muffin tin, greased or paper-lined

1. In a large bowl, combine whole-wheat flour, all-purpose flour, baking powder and salt. Make a well in the center.

2. In another bowl, whisk together egg, milk and oil. Add the honey. Stir into flour mixture until moist and lumpy.

3. Spoon batter into prepared muffin tin, dividing evenly. Bake in preheated oven for 20 to 25 minutes or until lightly browned.

Peanut Butter Wheat Muffins

1 1/4 cups	whole-wheat flour	300 mL
1 tsp	baking powder	5 mL
1 tsp	baking soda	5 mL
1/2 tsp	salt	2 mL
1/3 cup	packed brown sugar	75 mL
1	egg	1
1/2 cup	peanut butter	125 mL
1 cup	buttermilk	250 mL
1/2 tsp	vanilla	2 mL
1/2 cup	peanut halves (optional)	125 mL

Preheat oven to 400° F (200° C)
Muffin tin, greased or paper-lined

1. In a large bowl, mix together flour, baking powder, baking soda, salt and brown sugar. Make a well in the center.

2. In another bowl, whisk together egg and peanut butter. Whisk in milk and vanilla. Add to dry ingredients, stirring just until moistened.

3. Spoon batter into prepared muffin tin, filling cups three-quarters full. If desired, sprinkle with peanut halves. Bake in preheated oven for 15 to 18 minutes.

Raisin Bran Wheat Muffins

1 cup	wheat bran	250 mL
1 cup	buttermilk	250 mL
1/2 cup	raisins	125 mL
1/2 cup	honey	125 mL
1/4 cup	molasses	50 mL
1/3 cup	butter, melted *or* vegetable oil	75 mL
2	eggs	2
1 tsp	vanilla	5 mL
2 cups	whole-wheat flour	500 mL
1 tsp	baking powder	5 mL
1 tsp	baking soda	5 mL
1/4 tsp	cinnamon	1 mL
Pinch	salt	Pinch

Preheat oven to 400° F (200° C)
Muffin tin, greased or paper-lined

1. In a small bowl, combine bran, buttermilk and raisins. Set aside to soak.

2. In another bowl, whisk together honey, molasses, butter, eggs and vanilla. Add bran mixture.

3. In another bowl, sift together flour, baking powder, baking soda, cinnamon and salt. Add to liquid ingredients, stirring just until blended. Do not overmix.

4. Spoon batter into prepared muffin tin, filling cups to the top. Bake in preheated oven for 20 to 25 minutes.

HINT: Use baking soda to remove coffee and tea stains from plastic cups and dishes.

Apricot Bran Yogurt Muffins

1 1/4 cups	all-purpose flour	300 mL
1 1/4 cups	natural bran	300 mL
3/4 cup	packed brown sugar	175 mL
1 tbsp	baking powder	15 mL
1 tsp	baking soda	5 mL
1/4 tsp	cinnamon	1 mL
1/4 tsp	salt	1 mL
1 cup	chopped dried apricots	250 mL
1 cup	low-fat yogurt	250 mL
1/4 cup	vegetable oil	50 mL
1	egg	1
1 1/2 tsp	vanilla	7 mL

Preheat oven to 375° F (190° C)
Muffin tin, greased or paper-lined

1. In a large bowl, combine flour, bran, sugar, baking powder, baking soda, cinnamon and salt.

2. Set aside 2 tbsp (25 mL) of the apricots and add remaining apricots to flour mixture.

3. In another bowl, whisk together yogurt, oil, egg and vanilla. Add to flour mixture, stirring just until blended. Do not overmix.

4. Spoon batter into prepared muffin tin, filling cups three-quarters full. Sprinkle with reserved apricots. Bake in preheated oven for 20 to 25 minutes.

Blueberry Bran Yogurt Muffins

2 cups	yogurt	500 mL
2 tsp	baking soda	10 mL
1 1/2 cups	packed brown sugar	375 mL
2	eggs	2
1 cup	vegetable oil	250 mL
2 cups	natural bran	500 mL
2 tsp	vanilla	10 mL
2 cups	all-purpose flour	500 mL
4 tsp	baking powder	20 mL
1/2 tsp	salt	2 mL
1 cup	fresh blueberries *or* frozen blueberries, unsweetened	250 mL

Preheat oven to 350° F (180° C)
Muffin tin, greased or paper-lined

1. In a bowl combine yogurt and baking soda. Set aside.

2. In a large bowl, whisk together sugar, eggs and oil. Add bran and vanilla.

3. In another bowl, sift together flour, baking powder and salt. Add to bran mixture alternately with yogurt mixture. Fold in blueberries.

4. Spoon batter into prepared muffin tin, filling cups three-quarters full. Bake in preheated oven for 30 to 35 minutes or until toothpick inserted in center comes out clean.

HINT: When a recipe tells you to fold in egg whites, fruit or other ingredients, use a rubber spatula. Gently cut down through the center of the mixture, across the bottom and up the side, heaping mixture from bottom to top. Repeat, turning bowl slightly each time.

Orange-Glazed Yogurt Muffins

2 1/2 cups	all-purpose flour	625 mL
1 tsp	baking powder	5 mL
1 tsp	baking soda	5 mL
1/2 tsp	salt	2 mL
2/3 cup	butter *or* margarine	150 mL
2	eggs	2
1/2 cup	plain yogurt	125 mL
1/2 cup	orange juice	125 mL
1 tbsp	grated orange zest	15 mL

ORANGE GLAZE

3 to 4 tsp	orange juice	15 to 20 mL
1/2 cup	sifted icing sugar	125 mL

Preheat oven to 400° F (200° C)
Muffin tin, greased or paper-lined

1. In a bowl sift together flour, baking powder, baking soda and salt.

2. In a large mixer bowl, beat together butter and sugar until light and fluffy. Add eggs, yogurt, juice and zest, beating until smooth. Fold in flour mixture and stir just until blended. Do not overmix.

3. Spoon batter into prepared muffin tin, filling cups to the top. Bake in preheated oven for 15 to 20 minutes. Set aside to cool.

4. In a bowl combine juice and icing sugar to make a fairly thick glaze. Drizzle over cooled muffins.

Lemon Yogurt Cranberry Muffins

2/3 cup	honey	150 mL
1/3 cup	vegetable oil	75 mL
4	eggs	4
1 1/2 tsp	lemon extract	7 mL
1 3/4 cups	all-purpose flour	425 mL
3/4 cup	whole-wheat flour	175 mL
2 1/2 tsp	baking powder	12 mL
1 cup	lemon yogurt	250 mL
1 cup	coarsely chopped cranberries	250 mL
1 tbsp	grated lemon zest	15 mL

Preheat oven to 400° F (200° C)
Muffin tin, greased or paper-lined

1. In a large mixer bowl, beat together honey and oil until creamy. Beat in eggs and lemon extract.

2. In another bowl, combine all-purpose flour, whole-wheat flour and baking powder. Add to egg mixture alternately with yogurt, beginning and ending with flour mixture. Fold in cranberries and zest, stirring just until moistened. Do not overmix.

3. Spoon batter into prepared muffin tin, filling cups to the top. Bake in preheated oven for 15 to 20 minutes.

Special Muffin Treats

Afternoon Tea Muffins

1 1/2 cups	all-purpose flour	375 mL
1/2 cup	granulated sugar	125 mL
1/4 tsp	salt	1 mL
2 tsp	baking powder	10 mL
1 tsp	baking soda	5 mL
1 tsp	cinnamon	5 mL
1/2 tsp	ground nutmeg	2 mL
1 1/4 cups	raisins	300 mL
2	eggs, beaten	2
1 cup	buttermilk	250 mL
2 tbsp	margarine, melted	25 mL

Preheat oven to 400° F (200° C)
Muffin tin, greased or paper-lined

1. In a large bowl, mix together flour, sugar, salt, baking powder, baking soda, cinnamon and nutmeg. Fold in raisins.

2. In a small bowl, whisk together eggs, milk and margarine. Add to dry ingredients, stirring quickly just until moistened. Batter will be lumpy.

3. Spoon batter into prepared muffin tin, filling cups three-quarters full. Bake in preheated oven for 20 to 25 minutes.

Almond Citrus Muffins

1/2 cup	whole natural almonds	125 mL
1 1/4 cups	all-purpose flour	300 mL
2 tsp	baking powder	10 mL
1/4 tsp	salt	1 mL
1 cup	shredded wheat bran cereal	250 mL
1/4 cup	packed brown sugar	50 mL
3/4 cup	milk	175 mL
1/4 cup	orange juice	50 mL
1 tsp	grated orange zest	5 mL
1	egg	1
1/4 cup	vegetable oil *or* almond oil	50 mL

Preheat oven to 350° F (180° C)
Muffin tin, greased or paper-lined

1. Spread almonds in a single layer on baking sheet. Bake in preheated oven, stirring occasionally, for 12 to 15 minutes or until lightly toasted. Set aside to cool and then chop toasted almonds. Increase oven temperature to 400° F (200° C).

2. In a large bowl, combine flour, baking powder and salt.

3. In a medium bowl, combine cereal, sugar, milk, orange juice and zest. Let stand for 2 minutes or until cereal is softened. Add egg and oil, beating well. Stir in almonds. Add to flour mixture and stir until just moistened. Batter will be lumpy.

4. Spoon batter into prepared muffin tin. Bake in preheated oven for 20 minutes or until lightly browned.

Apple Almond Muffins

1/2 cup	butter (room temperature)	125 mL
1/2 cup	granulated sugar	125 mL
2 tsp	baking powder	10 mL
1/2 tsp	salt	2 mL
2	large eggs	2
2 cups	all-purpose flour	500 mL
1/2 cup	buttermilk	125 mL
1	can (8 oz [250 g]) almond paste	1
1 cup	chopped peeled apples	250 mL
	Thin apple slices	
	Warmed honey	

Preheat oven to 375° F (190° C)
Muffin tin, greased or paper-lined

1. In a large mixer bowl, beat together butter, sugar, baking powder and salt until pale and fluffy. Beat in eggs. Fold in flour alternately with buttermilk, beginning and ending with flour. Stir until well blended but do not overmix.

2. Crumble almond paste over batter and sprinkle with chopped apples. Stir just until blended.

3. Spoon batter into prepared muffin tin, filling cups two-thirds full. Top each with 2 thin slices of apple. Bake in preheated oven for 20 minutes or until a toothpick inserted in the center comes out dry and clean. Brush tops with 2 tbsp (25 mL) warmed honey.

Apple Cider Muffins

1/2 cup	packed brown sugar	125 mL
1/2 cup	vegetable oil	125 mL
1/4 cup	molasses	50 mL
1	egg	1
3/4 cup	sweet apple cider	175 mL
2	apples, peeled and finely chopped	2
1 1/2 cups	all-purpose flour	375 mL
3/4 cup	natural bran	175 mL
1 tbsp	baking powder	15 mL
1 tsp	baking soda	5 mL
1/2 tsp	salt	2 mL
1/2 tsp	ground nutmeg	2 mL
1 cup	raisins	250 mL
1/2 cup	chopped walnuts	125 mL

Preheat oven to 400° F (200° C)
Muffin tin, greased or paper-lined

1. In a bowl mix together sugar, oil, molasses and egg. Stir in cider and apples. Set aside.

2. In a large bowl, combine flour, bran, baking powder, baking soda, salt and nutmeg. Add apple mixture, stirring just until blended. Fold in raisins and walnuts.

3. Spoon batter into prepared muffin tin, filling cups three-quarters full. Bake in preheated oven for 15 to 20 minutes.

Striped Apple Cinnamon Muffins

2 cups	all-purpose flour	500 mL
1/4 cup	granulated sugar	50 mL
3 tsp	baking powder	15 mL
3/4 tsp	salt	4 mL
1/2 cup	finely chopped tart apple	125 mL
1	egg, beaten	1
3/4 cup	milk	175 mL
1/4 cup	vegetable oil	50 mL
TOPPING		
3 tbsp	granulated sugar	45 mL
1 tsp	cinnamon	5 mL
1/2 tsp	nutmeg	2 mL
1 cup	thinly sliced tart apple	250 mL

Preheat oven to 400° F (200° C)
Muffin tin, greased or paper-lined

1. In a large bowl, combine flour, sugar, baking powder and salt. Stir in chopped apple.

2. In another bowl, combine egg, milk and oil. Add to flour mixture and stir until just moistened and blended. Spoon batter into prepared muffin tin.

3. In a bowl mix together sugar, cinnamon and nutmeg. Coat apple slices with this topping and arrange slices over batter to make stripes. Bake in preheated oven for 20 to 25 minutes.

HINT: To prevent peeled or cut apples or other fruits from turning brown, brush surfaces with lemon juice.

Applesauce Crunch Muffins

1 1/2 cups	all-purpose flour	375 mL
1/4 cup	granulated sugar	50 mL
3 tsp	baking powder	15 mL
1/2 tsp	salt	2 mL
1/2 tsp	cinnamon	2 mL
1	egg	1
3/4 cup	milk	175 mL
3 tbsp	vegetable oil *or* shortening, melted	45 mL
	Applesauce	
TOPPING		
2/3 cup	lightly packed brown sugar	150 mL
1/3 cup	all-purpose flour	75 mL
2 tbsp	softened butter or margarine	25 mL

Preheat oven to 400° F (200° C)
Muffin tin, paper-lined

1. In a large bowl, sift together flour, sugar, baking powder, salt and cinnamon.

2. In another bowl, beat together egg, milk and oil. Pour into flour mixture. Stir just until moistened. Batter will be lumpy.

3. Spoon batter into prepared muffin tin, filling cups two-thirds full. Top each with 1 tsp (5 mL) applesauce.

4. In a small bowl, mix together brown sugar, flour and butter. Sprinkle over batter. Bake in preheated oven for 18 to 20 minutes or until golden brown.

Applesauce Snackin' Muffins

3/4 cup	all-purpose flour	175 mL
2/3 cup	whole-wheat flour	150 mL
3/4 tsp	baking soda	4 mL
1 tsp	cinnamon	5 mL
1/2 tsp	ground ginger	2 mL
Pinch	ground cloves	Pinch
1/8 tsp	salt	.5 mL
1 cup	applesauce	250 mL
1/4 cup	packed brown sugar	50 mL
1/4 cup	fancy molasses	50 mL
1/4 cup	vegetable oil	50 mL
2	eggs	2
1 cup	raisins	250 mL
	Icing (optional)	
2/3 cup	icing sugar	150 mL
1 tbsp	apple juice	15 mL

Preheat oven to 375° F (190° C)
Muffin tin, paper-lined

1. In a large bowl, combine all-purpose flour, whole-wheat flour, baking soda, cinnamon, ginger, cloves and salt.

2. In another bowl, whisk together applesauce, sugar, molasses, oil and eggs. Fold in raisins. Add to dry ingredients, stirring just until moistened and blended.

3. Spoon batter into prepared muffin tin, filling cups three-quarters full. Bake in preheated oven for 15 to 20 minutes.

4. In a bowl whisk together icing sugar and apple juice. Drizzle over cooled muffins.

Apricot Muffins

1 3/4 cups	all-purpose flour	425 mL
2 1/2 tsp	baking powder	12 mL
1/2 tsp	baking soda	2 mL
1/2 tsp	salt	2 mL
1/2 cup	chopped pecans	125 mL
2	eggs	2
1/4 cup	vegetable oil	50 mL
1/2 cup	lightly packed brown sugar	125 mL
1	can (14 oz [398 mL]) apricots, puréed	1
1 tsp	orange extract	5 mL

Preheat oven to 400° F (200° C)
Muffin tin, greased or paper-lined

1. In a large bowl, combine flour, baking powder, baking soda, salt and pecans.

2. In another bowl, beat eggs lightly. Add oil, brown sugar, puréed apricots and orange extract. Add to flour mixture, stirring just until blended. Batter will be lumpy.

3. Spoon batter into prepared muffin tin, filling cups to the top. Bake in preheated oven for 20 to 25 minutes.

HINT: Out of muffin pans? Use aluminum foil muffin or cupcake liners, or custard cups. Place on a cookie sheet and bake as usual.

Chocolate Chip Banana Muffins

2	ripe bananas, mashed	2
1 tsp	baking soda	5 mL
1 tsp	hot water	5 mL
1/2 cup	margarine *or* vegetable oil	125 mL
3/4 cup	granulated sugar	175 mL
1	egg, beaten	1
1 tsp	vanilla	5 mL
1 1/2 cups	all-purpose flour	375 mL
1 tsp	baking powder	5 mL
1 tsp	salt	5 mL
2/3 cup	chocolate chips	150 mL

Preheat oven to 425° F (220° C)
12-cup muffin tin, greased or paper-lined

1. In a bowl combine bananas, baking soda and hot water. Set aside.

2. In a large bowl, cream together margarine and sugar. Add egg and vanilla. Stir in flour, baking powder and salt, mixing until well blended. Add banana mixture and fold in chocolate chips.

3. Spoon batter into prepared muffin tin, filling cups three-quarters full. Bake in preheated oven for 15 to 20 minutes.

Corn Flakes n' Banana Muffins

1 1/4 cups	all-purpose flour	300 mL
1 tbsp	baking powder	15 mL
1/2 tsp	salt	2 mL
1/2 tsp	cinnamon	2 mL
1/4 tsp	ground nutmeg	1 mL
1/2 cup	firmly packed brown sugar	125 mL
2 cups	lightly crushed Corn Flakes	500 mL
1	egg	1
1/3 cup	milk	75 mL
1/4 cup	vegetable oil	50 mL
1 cup	mashed ripe bananas	250 mL

Preheat oven to 400° F (200° C)
Muffin tin, greased

1. In a medium bowl, sift together flour, baking powder, salt, cinnamon, nutmeg, brown sugar and crushed Corn Flakes.

2. In a large bowl, combine egg, milk and oil. Stir in banana. Add flour mixture and stir just until blended.

3. Spoon batter into prepared muffin tin, filling cups to the top. Bake in preheated oven for 20 to 25 minutes or until lightly brown.

HINT: Freeze ripe bananas for later use. Peel them and wrap in plastic wrap. Store them in freezer bags.

Banana Crumble Muffins

TOPPING

1/2 cup	Banana Nut Crunch cereal	125 mL
1 tbsp	packed brown sugar	15 mL
1 tsp	cinnamon	5 mL
1 tsp	vegetable oil	5 mL

1 1/4 cups	all-purpose flour	300 mL
1 tbsp	baking powder	15 mL
1/8 tsp	salt	0.5 mL
1	egg	1
1/2 cup	milk	125 mL
1/3 cup	firmly packed brown sugar	75 mL
3 tbsp	vegetable oil	45 mL
1 1/2 cups	Banana Nut Crunch cereal	375 mL
1 cup	finely chopped bananas	250 mL

Preheat oven to 400° F (200° C)
Muffin tin, greased or paper-lined

1. In a bowl mix together cereal, brown sugar and cinnamon. Drizzle with oil and mix until topping is crumbly. Set aside.

2. In a large bowl, combine flour, baking powder and salt. Make a well in the center.

3. In another bowl, whisk egg. Add milk, brown sugar and oil, blending well. Pour into flour mixture and stir just until moistened and blended. Do not overmix. Fold in cereal and bananas.

4. Spoon batter into prepared muffin tin, filling cups three-quarters full. Sprinkle with topping. Bake in preheated oven for 15 to 20 minutes or until lightly browned.

HINT: Ripen green bananas by wrapping in a wet dish towel and placing in a paper bag.

Berry Special Muffins

2 cups	all-purpose flour	500 mL
1/2 cup	granulated sugar	125 mL
1 1/2 tsp	baking powder	7 mL
1/2 tsp	baking soda	2 mL
1/2 tsp	salt	2 mL
1	egg	1
1/2 cup	orange juice	125 mL
1 1/2 tsp	grated orange zest	7 mL
1/2 cup	butter or margarine, melted	125 mL
1 cup	coarsely chopped fresh or frozen berries	250 mL

Preheat oven to 400° F (200° C)
Muffin tin, paper-lined

1. In a large bowl, combine flour, sugar, baking powder, baking soda and salt. Make a well in the center.

2. In another bowl, whisk together egg, orange juice, zest and margarine until well blended. Add to flour mixture and stir just until moistened and blended. Fold in berries.

3. Spoon batter into prepared muffin tin, filling cups to the top. Bake in preheated oven for 20 minutes or until golden brown.

Coffee Cake Blueberry Muffins

Preheat oven to 400° F (200° C)
12-cup muffin tin, greased or paper-lined

TOPPING		
2 tbsp	softened margarine	25 mL
1/2 cup	packed brown sugar	125 mL
1 1/2 tsp	cinnamon	7 mL
1 tbsp	all-purpose flour	15 mL

3/4 cup	softened margarine	175 mL
3/4 cup	granulated sugar	175 mL
1	egg	1
1 cup	sour cream	250 mL
1 tsp	vanilla	5 mL
2 cups	all-purpose flour	500 mL
1 tsp	baking powder	5 mL
1 tsp	baking soda	5 mL
1/4 tsp	salt	1 mL
2 cups	fresh blueberries *or* frozen blueberries, thawed and well drained	500 mL

1. In a small bowl, mix together margarine, brown sugar, cinnamon and flour. Set aside.

2. In a large mixer bowl, cream margarine and sugar until light and fluffy. Add egg and blend well on low speed. Stir in sour cream and vanilla. Add flour, baking powder, baking soda and salt. Stir just until moistened and blended.

3. Spoon batter into prepared muffin tin, filling cups half full. Add blueberries and top with remaining batter. Sprinkle with topping. Bake in preheated oven for 15 to 20 minutes or until golden brown.

Spiced Buttermilk Muffins

Preheat oven to 350° F (180° C)
Muffin tin, greased

2 cups	whole-wheat flour	500 mL
2/3 cup	all-purpose flour	150 mL
2/3 cup	packed brown sugar	150 mL
2 tsp	baking soda	10 mL
1 tsp	pumpkin pie spice	5 mL
2 cups	buttermilk	500 mL
3/4 cup	raisins	175 mL

1. In a large bowl, combine whole-wheat flour, all-purpose flour, sugar, baking soda and pumpkin pie spice. Add buttermilk, stirring just until moistened. Fold in raisins.

2. Spoon batter into prepared muffin tin, filling cups two-thirds full. Bake in preheated oven for 35 to 40 minutes or until toothpick inserted in center comes out clean and dry.

Blueberry Walnut Streusel Muffins

1 1/2 cups	all-purpose flour	375 mL
2 tsp	baking powder	10 mL
1/2 tsp	salt	2 mL
6 tbsp	softened butter	90 mL
1/2 cup	granulated sugar	125 mL
1	egg	1
1 tsp	vanilla	5 mL
1/2 cup	milk	125 mL
1 1/2 cups	fresh blueberries	375 mL
WALNUT STREUSEL TOPPING		
2 tbsp	melted butter	25 mL
2 tbsp	packed brown sugar	25 mL
1/4 tsp	cinnamon	1 mL
1/4 cup	chopped walnuts	50 mL

Preheat oven to 400° F (200° C)
Muffin tin, greased or paper-lined

1. In a medium bowl, combine flour, baking powder and salt.

2. In a large bowl, cream butter and sugar until light and fluffy. Beat in egg and vanilla. Add flour mixture alternately with milk. Stir just until moistened and blended. Fold in blueberries.

3. Spoon batter into prepared muffin tin, filling cups two-thirds full. In a bowl combine butter, brown sugar, cinnamon and walnuts. Sprinkle topping over batter. Bake in preheated oven for about 20 minutes.

Lemon Oat Blueberry Muffins

1 cup	all-purpose flour	250 mL
3 tsp	baking powder	15 mL
1/2 tsp	salt	2 mL
1/4 tsp	nutmeg	1 mL
3/4 cup	packed brown sugar	175 mL
3/4 cup	rolled oats	175 mL
	Finely grated zest of 1 lemon	
1	egg	1
1/4 cup	vegetable oil	50 mL
1 cup	milk	250 mL
1	can (14 oz [398 mL]) blueberries, drained and patted dry	1

Preheat oven to 400° F (200° C)
Muffin tin, greased or paper-lined

1. In a large bowl, combine flour, baking powder, salt, nutmeg and brown sugar. Stir with a fork until well blended. Add oats and lemon zest.

2. In another bowl, whisk together egg, oil and milk. Add to flour mixture, stirring just until blended and moistened. Fold in blueberries.

3. Spoon batter into prepared muffin tin, filling cups three-quarters full. Bake in preheated oven for 15 to 20 minutes.

Caramel Nut-Topped Muffins

Preheat oven to 400° F (200° C)
12-cup muffin tin

TOPPING

1/2 cup	firmly packed brown sugar	125 mL
1/4 cup	margarine	50 mL
1/2 cup	chopped pecans or walnuts	125 mL

2	eggs	2
3/4 cup	milk	175 mL
1/2 cup	margarine, melted	125 mL
1 1/2 cups	all-purpose flour	375 mL
1 cup	whole-wheat flour	250 mL
1/3 cup	granulated sugar	75 mL
1 tbsp	baking powder	15 mL
1 tsp	cinnamon	5 mL
1/2 tsp	salt	2 mL

1. Into each muffin cup, measure 2 tsp (10 mL) brown sugar and 1 tsp (5 mL) margarine. Place in preheated oven for 2 minutes to melt. Remove from oven and add 2 tsp (10 mL) nuts to each cup. Set aside.

2. In a bowl, beat eggs with a fork. Blend in milk and melted margarine.

3. In a large bowl, combine all-purpose flour, whole-wheat flour, sugar, baking powder, cinnamon and salt. Add liquid mixture, stirring just until moistened and blended. Do not overmix.

4. Spoon batter into muffin tin. Bake in preheated oven for about 20 minutes. Invert pan onto a plate so caramel nut topping is on top. Serve warm.

Cream Cheese Carrot Muffins

Preheat oven to 350° F (180° C)
12-cup muffin tin, greased or paper-lined

1	pkg (8 oz [250 g]) softened cream cheese	1
1/3 cup	granulated sugar	75 mL
1	egg	1
1 1/2 cups	all-purpose flour	375 mL
1 tsp	baking powder	5 mL
1 tsp	baking soda	5 mL
1/2 tsp	cinnamon	2 mL
1/2 cup	packed brown sugar	125 mL
1/3 cup	vegetable oil	75 mL
2	eggs	2
2/3 cup	plain yogurt	150 mL
1 cup	finely grated carrots	250 mL
1/2 cup	finely chopped walnuts	125 mL

1. In a small bowl, whisk together cream cheese, sugar and 1 egg. Set aside.

2. In a large bowl, combine flour, baking powder, baking soda and cinnamon.

3. In another bowl, combine brown sugar, oil, 2 eggs and yogurt. Stir in carrots and walnuts. Add to flour mixture and stir just until moistened.

4. Spoon about 2 tbsp (25 mL) batter into muffin tin. Top with heaping spoonfuls of cream cheese mixture and top with remaining batter. Bake in preheated oven for about 20 minutes.

Mini Cheesecakes

2	pkgs (8 oz [250 g] each) softened cream cheese	2
1/2 cup	granulated sugar	125 mL
1 tsp	vanilla	5 mL
2	eggs	2
12	vanilla wafers	12
	Jam, nuts, chocolate curls etc.	

Preheat oven to 325° F (160° C)
12-cup muffin tin, foil-lined

1. In a large mixer bowl, combine cheese, sugar and vanilla. Blend on medium speed until smooth. Add eggs, blending well.

2. Put 1 vanilla wafer in each cup. Spoon cheese mixture over wafers, filling cups three-quarters full. Bake in preheated oven for 25 minutes. Set aside to cool. Remove from tin and chill in refrigerator before serving. Top with whatever you like.

VARIATION

🧁 For a special flavor, use 1/2 tsp (2 mL) rum or almond flavoring in place of the vanilla.

Cheese Muffin Ring

1 1/2 cups	sifted cake flour	375 mL
2 tsp	baking powder	10 mL
1/2 tsp	salt	2 mL
3/4 cup	grated cheese (any type)	175 mL
1	egg, well beaten	1
1/2 cup	milk	125 mL
1 tbsp	butter or shortening, melted	15 mL

Preheat oven to 425° F (220° C)
Ring mold, greased

1. In a large bowl, sift together flour, baking powder and salt. Add cheese and blend together well.

2. In another bowl, combine egg, milk and melted butter. Add to dry ingredients, stirring just until moistened and blended.

3. Spoon batter into prepared ring mold. Bake in preheated oven for 25 minutes.

NOTE: Serve with scrambled eggs or vegetables.

Chocolate Cinnamon Muffins

1/2 cup	softened butter or margarine	125 mL
1/2 cup	granulated sugar	125 mL
2 tsp	baking powder	10 mL
1/2 tsp	salt	2 mL
2	eggs	2
2 cups	all-purpose flour	500 mL
1 tsp	cinnamon	5 mL
1/2 cup	buttermilk	125 mL
1 cup	melted semi-sweet chocolate chips	500 mL
4 oz	cream cheese, cut-up	125 g
2 tbsp	granulated sugar	25 mL
1/2 tsp	cinnamon	2 mL

Preheat oven to 375° F (190° C)
Muffin tin, greased or paper-lined

1. In a large mixer bowl, beat together butter, sugar, baking powder and salt until pale and fluffy. Beat in eggs.

2. In another bowl, mix together flour and cinnamon. Slowly stir into butter mixture alternately with buttermilk just until moistened and blended. Do not overmix. Fold in melted chocolate just until blended.

3. Spoon batter into prepared muffin tin, filling cups two-thirds full. Press pieces of cream cheese into top of batter in each cup. Sprinkle with sugar and cinnamon. Bake in preheated oven for about 20 minutes.

Mini Cinnamon Breakfast Muffins

1 1/2 cups	all-purpose flour	375 mL
1/2 cup	granulated sugar	125 mL
2 tsp	baking powder	10 mL
1/2 tsp	salt	2 mL
1/2 tsp	ground allspice	2 mL
1/2 tsp	ground nutmeg	2 mL
1	egg, lightly beaten	1
1/2 cup	milk (2% or skim)	125 mL
1/3 cup	butter or margarine, melted	75 mL

Preheat oven to 400° F (200° C)
Muffin tin, greased or paper-lined

1. In a large bowl, mix together flour, sugar, baking powder, salt, allspice and nutmeg. Make a well in the center.

2. In another bowl, combine egg, milk and margarine, beating until well blended. Add to dry ingredients, stirring only until moistened and blended. Do not overmix.

3. Spoon batter into prepared muffin tin, filling cups to the top. Bake in preheated oven for 12 to 14 minutes or until muffins are done.

NOTE: For an extra delicious muffin, melt 1/4 cup (50 mL) margarine and brush over tops of warm muffins. Mix together 1/2 tsp (2 mL) cinnamon and 2 tbsp (25 mL) sugar and sprinkle over tops.

Morning Glory Corn Muffins

1 cup	all-purpose flour	250 mL
3/4 cup	yellow cornmeal	175 mL
3 tbsp	granulated sugar	45 mL
1 tbsp	double-acting baking powder	15 mL
1 tsp	salt	5 mL
1	egg	1
3/4 cup	milk	175 mL
1/3 cup	butter or margarine, melted	75 mL

Preheat oven to 400° F (200° C)
Muffin tin, greased or paper-lined

1. In a large bowl with a fork, combine flour, cornmeal, sugar, baking powder and salt. Make a well in the center.

2. In another bowl with a fork, mix together egg, milk and butter. Add to flour mixture, stirring just until flour is moistened. Do not overmix.

3. Spoon batter into prepared muffin tin, filling cups three-quarters full. Bake in preheated oven for 20 minutes or until lightly browned.

Kernel Krunch Corn Muffins

3/4 cup	softened unsalted butter	175 mL
3/4 cup	granulated sugar	175 mL
3	large eggs	3
1 2/3 cups	all-purpose flour	400 mL
1 2/3 cups	yellow cornmeal	400 mL
4 tsp	baking powder	20 mL
1/2 tsp	salt	2 mL
2 cups	milk	500 mL
1 cup	drained whole corn kernels	250 mL

Preheat oven to 425° F (220° C)
Muffin tin, greased or paper-lined

1. In a large bowl, cream together butter and sugar until fluffy. Beat in eggs one at a time, beating well after each addition.

2. In another bowl, mix together flour, cornmeal, baking powder and salt. Add to creamed mixture alternately with milk, mixing on low speed, beginning and ending with dry ingredients. Fold in corn.

3. Spoon batter into prepared muffin tin, filling cups to the top. Bake in preheated oven for 20 minutes.

HINT: Never double the amount of salt when you double a recipe. Season according to taste.

Old-Fashioned Corn Bread Muffins

1 1/2 cups	yellow cornmeal	375 mL
1 1/2 tsp	baking powder	7 mL
1 tsp	salt	5 mL
3/4 tsp	baking soda	4 mL
1	egg	1
1 1/2 cups	buttermilk	375 mL
1/4 cup	shortening, melted	50 mL

Preheat oven to 425° F (220° C)
12-cup muffin tin, greased

1. In a large bowl, combine cornmeal, baking powder, salt and baking soda until well blended. Make a well in the center.

2. In another bowl, beat together egg and buttermilk. Add to dry ingredients, stirring until thin and smooth. Stir in melted shortening.

3. Heat muffin tin in preheated oven. Spoon batter into hot tin and then bake for 18 to 20 minutes or until crusty and golden brown. Serve hot.

NOTE: These are made with cornmeal only, no flour. It makes them crispy outside and moist inside.

Cranberry Upside-Down Muffins

3/4 cup	whole berry cranberry sauce	175 mL
1/4 cup	chopped pecans	50 mL
2 tbsp	granulated sugar	25 mL
1/4 tsp	ground nutmeg	1 mL
12	pecan halves	12
1/2 cup	butter or margarine (room temperature)	125 mL
1/2 cup	granulated sugar	125 mL
2 tsp	baking powder	10 mL
1/2 tsp	salt	2 mL
2	large eggs	2
2 cups	all-purpose flour	500 mL
1/2 cup	buttermilk	125 mL

Preheat oven to 375° F (190° C)
12-cup muffin tin, greased

1. In a bowl mix together cranberry sauce, chopped pecans, sugar and nutmeg. Divide evenly amongst muffin tin cups. Press 1 pecan half into center of each cup. Set aside.

2. In a large mixer bowl, beat together butter, sugar, baking powder and salt until pale and fluffy. Beat in eggs. Gently stir in flour alternately with buttermilk, beginning and ending with flour.

3. Spoon batter gently over cranberry mixture, filling cups to the top. Bake in preheated oven for about 20 minutes Cool slightly and then invert muffin pan over a plate.

HINT: Add a few teaspoons of sugar and cinnamon to an empty pie plate and slowly burn over the stove. Your home will smell like a bakery.

Creamy Muffin Curls

2 cups	all-purpose flour	500 mL
4 tsp	baking powder	20 mL
1/2 tsp	salt	2 mL
4 tbsp	shortening	60 mL
2/3 cup	milk	150 mL
3 tbsp	creamed butter	45 mL
1/2 cup	packed brown sugar	125 mL

Preheat oven to 375° F (190° C)
Muffin tin, greased

1. In a large bowl with a fork, mix together flour, baking powder and salt. Add shortening and then milk, blending to make a soft dough. Knead slightly and then roll out to 1/4 inch (5 mm) thick.

2. Spread with creamed butter and sprinkle with brown sugar. Roll up like a jelly roll. Cut into 1-inch (2.5 cm) pieces. Stand rolls on end in prepared muffin tin. Bake in preheated oven for 30 minutes.

NOTE: Centers of rolls curl up and will be glazed on edges.

Cinnamon Coffee Cake Muffins

1/4 cup	all-purpose flour	50 mL
2 tbsp	granulated sugar	25 mL
1/2 tsp	cinnamon	2 mL
2 tbsp	butter *or* margarine	25 mL
1 1/3 cups	all-purpose flour	325 mL
1 cup	whole-wheat flour	250 mL
1/2 cup	packed brown sugar	125 mL
1 tbsp	baking powder	15 mL
1 tbsp	cinnamon	15 mL
1/2 tsp	salt	2 mL
1/3 cup	butter *or* margarine	75 mL
2	eggs	2
1 1/2 cups	milk	375 mL
1/2 cup	raisins	125 mL

Preheat oven to 400° F (200° C)
Muffin tin, greased or paper-lined

1. In a small bowl, mix together flour, sugar and cinnamon. With a pastry blender or 2 knives, cut in 2 tbsp (25 mL) butter until mixture resembles coarse crumbs. Set aside.

2. In a large bowl, combine all-purpose flour, whole-wheat flour, brown sugar, baking powder, cinnamon and salt. Cut in butter. Make a well in the center.

3. In another bowl, whisk together eggs and milk until blended. Add to flour mixture, stirring only until moistened. Fold in raisins.

4. Spoon batter into prepared muffin tin, filling cups only half full. Add 1 tbsp (15 mL) filling to each and top with remaining batter. Sprinkle any remaining filling on top. Bake in preheated oven for 20 minutes or until firm to the touch.

NOTE: Cutting in butter produces a lighter, cake-like texture in these muffins.

Island Fruit Muffins

2 1/4 cups	oat bran	550 mL
2/3 cup	all-purpose flour	150 mL
2/3 cup	whole-wheat flour	150 mL
1 tsp	baking powder	5 mL
2 1/2 tsp	baking soda	12 mL
1/4 tsp	salt	1 mL
1 1/2 cups	golden raisins	375 mL
1 1/4 cups	shredded coconut	300 mL
2	eggs	2
1 cup	buttermilk	250 mL
1/2 cup	vegetable oil	125 mL
1 cup	mashed bananas	250 mL
1/2 cup	honey	125 mL

Preheat oven to 375° F (190° C)
Muffin tin, greased or paper-lined

1. In a large bowl, combine oat bran, all-purpose flour, whole-wheat flour, baking powder, baking soda, salt, raisins and coconut.

2. In another bowl, whisk together eggs, buttermilk, oil, bananas and honey. Add to dry ingredients, stirring just until moistened and blended. Do not overmix.

3. Spoon batter into prepared muffin tin, filling cups three-quarters full. Bake in preheated oven for 20 to 25 minutes or until browned.

HINT: To tint coconut, place 1 1/3 cups (325 mL) flaked coconut in a jar. Add a few drops of food coloring, screw on lid and shake well.

Fresh Fruit Muffins

2 cups	all-purpose flour	500 mL
1/2 cup	granulated sugar	125 mL
1/3 cup	skim milk powder	75 mL
1 tbsp	baking powder	15 mL
1/2 tsp	salt	2 mL
1	egg	1
1/2 cup	margarine, melted	125 mL
1/2 cup	milk (2% or skim)	125 mL
1 cup	chopped fresh fruit	250 mL
1 tsp	lemon juice	5 mL
1/2 tsp	grated lemon zest	2 mL

Preheat oven to 400° F (200° C)
12-cup muffin tin, lightly greased

1. In a large bowl, combine flour, sugar, skim milk powder, baking powder and salt.

2. In another bowl, whisk together egg, margarine and milk until blended. Add fruit, lemon juice and zest. Add to flour mixture, stirring just until blended. Batter will be lumpy.

3. Spoon batter evenly into prepared muffin tin. Bake in preheated oven for 15 to 20 minutes or until golden brown.

HINT: The key to tender muffins is not to overmix. Just mix ingredients until no flour is visible.

Lemon Berry Streusel Muffins

1/4 cup	butter or margarine, melted	50 mL
1/2 cup	all-purpose flour	125 mL
2 tbsp	granulated sugar	25 mL
1 1/2 tsp	finely grated lemon zest	7 mL
2 1/2 cups	all-purpose flour	625 mL
2 tsp	baking powder	10 mL
1 tsp	baking soda	5 mL
1 1/4 cups	granulated sugar	300 mL
1 tbsp	finely shredded lemon	15 mL
1	egg	1
1 cup	buttermilk	250 mL
1/2 cup	butter or margarine, melted	125 mL
1 tbsp	lemon juice	15 mL
1 1/2 cups	frozen berries (any kind), coated with 1 tbsp (15 mL) flour	375 mL

Preheat oven to 400° F (200° C)
Muffin tin, paper-lined

1. In a bowl mix together butter, flour, sugar and zest. Set aside.

2. In a large bowl, combine flour, baking powder, baking soda, sugar and lemon zest.

3. In another bowl, whisk together egg, buttermilk, melted butter and lemon juice. Add to dry ingredients, stirring just until moistened and blended. Fold in berries.

4. Spoon batter into prepared muffin tin, filling cups two-thirds full. Crumble reserved topping over tops. Bake in preheated oven for 20 minutes or until lightly browned.

Lemon Pepper Muffins

2 cups	all-purpose flour	500 mL
1/2 cup	granulated sugar	125 mL
2 tsp	baking powder	10 mL
1/2 tsp	baking soda	2 mL
1/2 tsp	salt	2 mL
3/4 tsp	freshly ground black pepper	4 mL
	Finely grated zest of 1 lemon	
1 cup	milk	250 mL
	Juice of 1 lemon	
1	egg	1
1/3 cup	butter, melted	75 mL

Preheat oven to 400° F (200° C)
Muffin tin, greased or paper-lined

1. In a large bowl, combine flour, sugar, baking powder, baking soda, salt and pepper. Stir until well blended. Add lemon zest and mix until well coated. Make a well in the center.

2. In another bowl, whisk together milk, lemon juice and egg. Add to dry ingredients at once. (Milk mixture may look curdled.) Stir just until well blended. Add butter and blend together.

3. Spoon batter into prepared muffin tin, filling cups three-quarters full. Bake in preheated oven for 15 to 20 minutes or until toothpick inserted in center comes out clean.

HINT: Freeze grated zest from lemons and oranges in small plastic yogurt cups.

Mexican Muffins

1 cup	milk	250 mL
1/4 cup	butter, melted	50 mL
2	eggs, beaten	2
2 cups	all-purpose flour	500 mL
2 tsp	baking powder	10 mL
2 tsp	ground cumin	10 mL
1/2 tsp	salt	2 mL
1/2 cup	chopped fresh cilantro	125 mL

Preheat oven to 400° F (200° C)
Muffin tin, greased

1. In a medium bowl, whisk together milk, butter and eggs.

2. In another bowl, combine flour, baking powder, cumin and salt. Add to milk mixture and stir just until blended. Stir in cilantro.

3. Spoon batter into prepared muffin tin, filling cups to the top. Bake in preheated oven about 15 minutes or until toothpick inserted in center comes out clean and dry.

Mocha Walnut Frosted Muffins

1/2 cup	softened butter or margarine	125 mL
1 cup	granulated sugar	250 mL
2 cups	all-purpose flour	500 mL
3 tsp	baking powder	15 mL
1/4 tsp	salt	1 mL
1/2 cup	cold strong coffee	125 mL
3/4 cup	chopped walnuts	175 mL
3	egg whites, stiffly beaten	3
FROSTING		
3 tbsp	softened butter	45 mL
1 cup	icing sugar	250 mL
1 tbsp	powdered cocoa	15 mL
2 tbsp	strong coffee	25 mL

Preheat oven to 350° F (180° C)
Muffin tin, greased or paper-lined

1. In a large bowl, cream butter thoroughly. Add sugar gradually, beating well.

2. In another bowl, mix together flour, baking powder and salt. Add to creamed mixture alternately with coffee. Stir thoroughly until well blended. Add chopped walnuts. Fold in egg whites.

3. Spoon batter into prepared muffin tin, filling cups two-thirds full. Bake in preheated oven for 25 minutes.

4. In a bowl cream together butter and 2 tbsp (25 mL) icing sugar. Add coffee, remaining icing and cocoa. Beat until light and fluffy. Spread over cooled muffins.

NOTE: To make icing with a smooth glazed surface, use liquid hot.

Cocoa Nut Oatmeal Muffins

1/2 cup	margarine, melted	125 mL
2	eggs	2
1 cup	milk	250 mL
1 tsp	vanilla	5 mL
1 1/4 cups	all-purpose flour	300 mL
3/4 cup	oats	175 mL
1 cup	granulated sugar	250 mL
1/3 cup	cocoa	75 mL
1 tbsp	baking powder	15 mL
1 tsp	salt	5 mL
1 cup	chopped nuts	250 mL

Preheat oven to 400° F (200° C)
Muffin tin, greased or paper-lined

1. In a small bowl, whisk together margarine, eggs, milk and vanilla.

2. In a large bowl, mix together flour, oats, sugar, cocoa, baking powder and salt. Add egg mixture, stirring just until moistened and blended. Fold in chopped nuts.

3. Spoon batter into prepared muffin tin, filling cups to the top. Bake in preheated oven for 15 to 20 minutes or until toothpick inserted in the center comes out clean and dry.

HINT: Try ice cream muffins! Soften 2 or 3 different flavors of ice cream. Fill muffin tins one-third full with one flavor. Smooth out into bottoms of cups and then layer with the other flavors. Freeze, unmold and then decorate as you wish.

Almond Orange Muffins

2 1/4 cups	all-purpose flour	550 mL
1/2 cup	granulated sugar	125 mL
2 1/2 tsp	baking powder	12 mL
1/2 tsp	baking soda	2 mL
1/4 cup	sliced almonds	50 mL
1/2 cup	skim milk	125 mL
1/2 cup	orange juice	125 mL
1/4 cup	butter or margarine, melted	50 mL
2	egg whites	2
1 tsp	grated orange zest	5 mL

Preheat oven to 375° F (190° C)
Muffin tin, lightly greased or paper-lined

1. In a large bowl, combine flour, sugar, baking powder and baking soda. Stir in almonds.

2. In a small bowl, combine milk, orange juice, melted butter, egg whites and orange zest. Mix until well blended. Add to flour mixture, stirring lightly just until moistened and blended. Batter will be lumpy.

3. Spoon batter into prepared muffin tin, dividing equally. Bake in preheated oven for 15 to 20 minutes.

Miniature Orange-Dipped Muffins

1/2 cup	softened butter	125 mL
1 cup	granulated sugar	250 mL
2 cups	all-purpose flour	500 mL
1 tsp	baking soda	5 mL
1 tsp	salt	5 mL
1 tsp	grated orange zest	5 mL
3/4 cup	sour cream	175 mL
1/2 cup	raisins	125 mL
1/2 cup	chopped nuts	125 mL
DIP		
1 cup	granulated sugar	250 mL
1/2 cup	orange juice	125 mL

Preheat oven to 375° F (190° C)
Miniature muffin tins, well-greased

1. In a large bowl, cream together butter and sugar until smooth.

2. In another bowl, combine flour, baking soda, salt and zest. Add to creamed mixture alternately with sour cream, stirring just until blended. Do not overmix. Fold in raisins and chopped nuts.

3. Spoon batter into prepared muffin tins. Bake in preheated oven for 12 to 15 minutes.

4. In a bowl combine sugar and orange juice. Dip warm muffins into this mixture.

HINT: Soften butter quickly by grating it.

Here's another way to make a delicious dessert using orange cups instead of muffin tins or custard cups.

Orange Sunbursts

5	oranges	5
1/2 cup	snipped dates	125 mL
1/4 cup	flaked coconut	50 mL
Dash	aromatic bitters	Dash
	Marshmallows	

Preheat oven to 325° F (160° C)
Oblong baking dish

1. Cut tops off oranges with a grapefruit knife. Scoop out pulp and chop.

2. In a bowl combine pulp, dates, coconut and bitters. Spoon mixture into orange shells and place in baking dish. Pour a little water around oranges.

3. Bake in preheated oven for 25 minutes. Top each orange with a marshmallow and continue baking for 8 to 10 minutes or until marshmallows are golden.

HINT: To cut sticky ingredients like prunes, dates or marshmallows, dip kitchen shears in hot water often, or rub the blades with vegetable oil.

Spicy Orange and Sweet Potato Muffins

1 cup	all-purpose flour	250 mL
1 cup	whole-wheat flour	250 mL
2 tsp	baking powder	10 mL
2 tsp	baking soda	10 mL
1 tsp	cinnamon	5 mL
1/2 tsp	ground nutmeg	2 mL
1/2 tsp	ground allspice	2 mL
1	can (16 oz [455 mL]) sweet potatoes, drained	1
2/3 cup	firmly packed brown sugar	150 mL
2	eggs	2
1 cup	orange juice	250 mL
1	carrot, shredded	1
1 tsp	vanilla	5 mL

Preheat oven to 400° F (200° C)
Muffin tin, greased or paper-lined

1. In a medium bowl, combine all-purpose flour, whole-wheat flour, baking powder, baking soda, cinnamon, nutmeg and allspice.

2. In a large bowl, mash sweet potatoes. Add brown sugar, eggs, orange juice, carrot and vanilla. Mix together until well blended. Add flour mixture, stirring just until moistened and blended. Do not overmix.

3. Spoon batter into prepared muffin tin, filling cups to the top. Bake in preheated oven for 15 to 20 minutes or until golden brown. Serve warm.

HINT: For long-term storage of eggs, crack them open into an ice-cube tray. When completely frozen, put egg cubes in a sealed freezer bag and use as needed.

Orange Tea Muffins

1 1/2 cups	all-purpose flour	375 mL
1/2 cup	granulated sugar	125 mL
2 tsp	baking powder	10 mL
1/2 tsp	salt	2 mL
1/2 cup	butter or margarine, melted	125 mL
	Grated zest of 1 orange	
1/2 cup	fresh orange juice	125 mL
2	eggs	2
1 cup	fresh or frozen raspberries (optional)	250 mL
1/2 cup	sweetened flaked coconut (optional)	125 mL

Preheat oven to 375° F (190° C)
12-cup muffin tin, greased or paper-lined

1. In a large bowl, combine flour, sugar, baking powder and salt.

2. In another bowl, combine melted butter, orange zest, orange juice and eggs, mixing well. If desired, add raspberries and coconut. Add to flour mixture, stirring just until moist and blended.

3. Spoon batter into prepared muffin tin, dividing evenly. Bake in preheated oven for 15 to 20 minutes (22 to 25 if using raspberries and coconut) or until lightly browned.

Peanut Butter Surprise Muffins

1 cup	all-purpose flour	250 mL
1/2 tsp	salt	2 mL
3 tsp	baking powder	15 mL
1 tbsp	granulated sugar	15 mL
1/2 cup	cornmeal	125 mL
1 cup	milk	250 mL
1	egg, beaten	1
1/4 cup	peanut butter	50 mL
1 tbsp	shortening, melted	15 mL

1. In a large bowl, combine flour, salt, baking powder and sugar. Stir in cornmeal, mixing to blend well.

2. In a small bowl, combine milk, egg, peanut butter and melted shortening. Add to dry ingredients, stirring until moistened and blended.

3. Spoon batter into prepared muffin tin, filling cups three-quarters full. Bake in preheated oven for about 20 minutes.

MOCHA WALNUT FROSTED MUFFINS (PAGE 157) ➤

Cinnamon Pear Muffins

3 cups	diced peeled pears	750 mL
3/4 cup	granulated sugar	175 mL
1/2 cup	vegetable oil	125 mL
2	eggs	2
2 tsp	vanilla	10 mL
2 cups	all-purpose flour	500 mL
2 tsp	baking soda	10 mL
2 tsp	cinnamon	10 mL
1 tsp	ground nutmeg	5 mL
1 tsp	salt	5 mL
1 cup	raisins	250 mL
1 cup	chopped walnuts or pecans	250 mL

Preheat oven to 400° F (200° C)
Muffin tin, greased or paper-lined

1. In a bowl combine pears and sugar.

2. In a large bowl, whisk together oil, eggs and vanilla. Add pear mixture and blend well.

3. In another bowl, combine flour, baking soda, cinnamon, nutmeg and salt. Add to oil mixture and stir just until moistened and blended. Do not overmix. Fold in raisins and walnuts.

4. Spoon batter into prepared muffin tin, filling cups to the top. Bake in preheated oven for about 20 minutes.

HINT: Check spices for freshness by sniffing for aroma. The stronger the aroma, the fresher and more flavorful they will be.

Potato Pudding Muffins

12	medium potatoes	12
2	grated medium onions	2
4	eggs, well-beaten	4
1 cup	all-purpose flour	250 mL
1 tbsp	salt	15 mL
1/2 tsp	pepper	2 mL
1/2 tsp	savory	2 mL
1 tsp	baking powder	5 mL
8 tbsp	bacon fat or butter, melted	125 mL

Preheat oven to 375° F (190° C)
Muffin tin, lightly greased

1. Peel potatoes and grate over a bowl of cold water. Drain, pressing out as much water as possible. In a large bowl, combine grated potatoes, onions and eggs.

2. In another bowl, combine flour, salt, pepper, savory and baking powder. Add to potato mixture and mix well. Stir in melted fat.

3. Spoon batter into prepared muffin tin, filling cups to the top. Bake in preheated oven for 1 hour or until brown and crusty. Let stand for 30 minutes on a cake rack, then run a knife around edges and remove from pan.

NOTE: To freeze, place muffins on a baking sheet, freeze, and then put into freezer bags.

◄ (CLOCKWISE FROM UPPER RIGHT): APPLE AND PLUM BUTTER (PAGE 171), ORANGE MARMALADE (PAGE 176), STRAWBERRY RHUBARB JAM (PAGE 174)

Creamy Pumpkin Nut Muffins

CREAM CHEESE FILLING

4 oz	softened cream cheese	115 mL
2 tbsp	packed brown sugar	25 mL
1 1/2 tsp	maple flavoring	7 mL

MUFFINS

2 cups	all-purpose flour	500 mL
3/4 cup	packed brown sugar	175 mL
1/2 cup	chopped walnuts	125 mL
2 tsp	baking powder	10 mL
1 tsp	cinnamon	5 mL
1/2 tsp	baking soda	2 mL
1/4 tsp	salt	1 mL
2	eggs	2
1 cup	pumpkin purée	250 mL
3/4 cup	evaporated milk	175 mL
1/4 cup	vegetable oil	50 mL
2 tsp	maple flavoring	10 mL

NUT TOPPING

2 tbsp	packed brown sugar	25 mL
1/4 cup	chopped walnuts	50 mL

Preheat oven to 400° F (200° C)
Muffin tin, greased or paper-lined

1. In a bowl mix together cream cheese, brown sugar and maple flavoring until smooth. Set aside.

2. In a large bowl, mix together flour, sugar, nuts, baking powder, cinnamon, baking soda and salt. Make a well in the center.

3. In another bowl, whisk together eggs, pumpkin, evaporated milk, oil and maple flavoring until well blended. Add to flour mixture, stirring just until moistened and blended. Do not overmix.

4. Spoon batter into prepared muffin tin, filling cups two-thirds full. Add 1 heaping tsp (5 mL) cream cheese filling to each cup. Sprinkle with brown sugar and walnuts. Bake in preheated oven for about 20 minutes.

HINT: To keep a bowl from slipping on a working surface, place it on a folded wet towel.

Raspberry Corn Muffins

3/4 cup	fresh raspberries	175 mL
1 1/2 cups	all-purpose flour	375 mL
3/4 cup	granulated sugar	175 mL
3/4 cup	yellow cornmeal	175 mL
1 tbsp	baking powder	15 mL
1/2 tsp	salt	2 mL
2	eggs	2
1 cup	milk	250 mL
1 tsp	vanilla	5 mL
4 tbsp	melted butter	60 mL

Preheat oven to 400° F (200° C)
12-cup muffin tin, lightly greased

1. In a small bowl, gently toss together raspberries and 2 tbsp (25 mL) flour.

2. In a large bowl, combine remaining flour, sugar, cornmeal, baking powder and salt. Make a well in the center.

3. In another bowl, whisk together eggs, milk and vanilla. Add to dry ingredients along with melted butter. Stir quickly just to moisten and blend.

4. Spoon 2 tbsp (25 mL) batter into each prepared muffin cup. Scatter 3 or 4 floured raspberries into each cup and spoon remaining batter over top. Bake in preheated oven for 15 minutes or until golden brown.

Kiwi Raspberry Muffins

1 cup	all-purpose flour	250 mL
1 cup	whole-wheat flour	250 mL
1 tbsp	baking powder	15 mL
1/2 tsp	baking soda	2 mL
2	peeled chopped kiwi	2
1/2 cup	fresh raspberries (or frozen)	125 mL
1	egg, lightly beaten	1
1/4 cup	margarine *or* butter	50 mL
1/3 cup	skim milk	75 mL
1 tsp	vanilla	5 mL

Preheat oven to 400° F (200° C)
Muffin tin, greased or paper-lined

1. In a large bowl, mix together all-purpose flour, whole-wheat flour, baking powder and baking soda. Add kiwi and raspberries, mixing well. Make a well in the center.

2. In another bowl, combine egg, margarine, milk and vanilla. Add to the flour mixture, stirring only until moistened and blended. Do not over-mix.

3. Spoon batter into prepared muffin tin, filling cups to the top. Bake in preheated oven for 15 to 20 minutes.

Smoked Sausage Corn Muffins

8 oz	smoked sausage	250 g
1 cup	all-purpose flour	250 mL
3/4 cup	yellow cornmeal	175 mL
1/4 cup	granulated sugar	50 mL
1 tbsp	baking powder	15 mL
1 cup	buttermilk	250 mL
1/4 cup	vegetable oil	50 mL
2	eggs, beaten	2

Preheat oven to 375° F (190° C)
Muffin tin, paper-lined

1. Cut sausage into quarters lengthwise, then cut crosswise into 1/4-inch (5 mm) pieces. In a skillet over medium heat, lightly brown sausage. Remove from skillet and drain on paper towels.

2. In a large bowl, combine flour, cornmeal, sugar and baking powder. Add buttermilk, oil, eggs and sausage, stirring just until blended.

3. Spoon batter into prepared muffin tin, filling cups three-quarters full. Bake in preheated oven for 15 minutes or until golden brown.

NOTE: Delicious with scrambled eggs in place of toast.

Salmon Lunch Muffins

1	can (6 oz [175 mL]) skinless, boneless salmon, not drained	1
2	eggs	2
1/2 cup	chopped celery	125 mL
1/2 cup	quick-cooking rolled oats	125 mL
1/2 tsp	baking powder	2 mL
1/4 cup	evaporated milk	50 mL
2 tsp	lemon juice	10 mL
3/4 tsp	salt	4 mL
1/4 tsp	black pepper	1 mL

Preheat oven to 350° F (180° C)
6-cup muffin tin, lightly greased

1. In a food processor, combine salmon (and juice), eggs, celery, oats, baking powder, milk, lemon juice, salt and pepper. Purée until well blended.

2. Spoon batter into prepared muffin tin, dividing evenly. Bake in preheated oven for 30 minutes or until golden brown. Serve warm.

NOTE: For a tangier muffin, add 1 or 2 drops of Tabasco sauce.

HINT: Run a cut-up lemon (or other citrus fruit) through your garbage disposal to freshen the air in your kitchen.

Gingerbread Sour Cream Muffins

1 1/2 cups	all-purpose flour	375 mL
1 tsp	baking soda	5 mL
1 tsp	ground ginger	5 mL
1/4 tsp	salt	1 mL
2	eggs	2
1/2 cup	sour cream	125 mL
1/2 cup	molasses	125 mL
1/4 cup	packed brown sugar	50 mL
1/4 cup	butter or margarine, melted	50 mL
	Sweetened whipped cream *or* lemon sauce	

Preheat oven to 400° F (200° C)
Muffin tin, greased

1. In a medium bowl, combine flour, baking soda, ginger and salt.

2. In a large bowl, beat eggs with a fork until light. Add sour cream, molasses, sugar and butter, blending well. Add flour mixture, stirring just until moistened and blended.

3. Spoon batter into prepared muffin tin, filling cups three-quarters full. Bake in preheated oven for 15 to 20 minutes. Serve warm topped with whipped cream or lemon sauce.

HINT: No whipped cream? Beat egg whites until stiff and add 1 sliced banana per egg white. Beat again until bananas are dissolved.

Sweet Potato Muffins

2/3 cup	cooked sweet potatoes, well-drained	150 mL
1/4 cup	butter *or* margarine	50 mL
1/2 cup	granulated sugar	125 mL
1	egg	1
3/4 cup	all-purpose flour	175 mL
2 tsp	baking powder	10 mL
1/2 tsp	salt	2 mL
1/2 tsp	cinnamon	2 mL
1/4 tsp	ground nutmeg	1 mL
1/2 cup	milk	125 mL
1/4 cup	chopped pecans or walnuts	50 mL
1/4 cup	chopped raisins	50 mL

Preheat oven to 400° F (200° C)
Muffin tin, greased

1. In a blender or food processor, purée sweet potatoes.

2. In a large bowl, cream together butter and sugar. Beat in egg and puréed sweet potatoes.

3. In another bowl, combine flour, baking powder, salt, cinnamon and nutmeg. Add to sweet potato mixture alternately with milk and mix just until moistened and blended. Fold in chopped nuts and raisins.

4. Spoon batter into prepared muffin tin, filling cups three-quarters full. If desired, sprinkle with sugar and cinnamon. Bake in preheated oven for about 20 minutes.

Strawberry Pecan Muffins

1/4 cup	all-purpose flour	50 mL
1/4 cup	finely chopped pecans	50 mL
1/4 cup	light brown sugar	50 mL
2 tbsp	softened butter or margarine	25 mL

2 cups	all-purpose flour	500 mL
1/3 cup	granulated sugar	75 mL
2 1/2 tsp	baking powder	12 mL
1 tsp	grated lemon zest	5 mL
1/4 tsp	salt	1 mL
2/3 cup	milk	150 mL
1/4 cup	butter or margarine, melted	50 mL
1	egg	1
2 cups	finely chopped fresh strawberries	500 mL

Preheat oven to 400° F (200° C)
Muffin tin, paper-lined

1. In a small bowl, combine flour, pecans, brown sugar and softened butter. Mix with your fingers until crumbly. Set aside.

2. In a large bowl, combine flour, sugar, baking powder, lemon zest and salt. Make a well in the center.

3. In another bowl, whisk together milk, melted butter and egg until blended. Add to flour mixture and stir just until moistened. Do not overmix. The batter will be lumpy. Fold in strawberries.

4. Spoon batter into prepared muffin tin, filling cups two-thirds full. Sprinkle with streusel topping. Bake in preheated oven for 20 to 25 minutes.

HINT: Save margarine tubs for storing baking ingredients such as raisins, cinnamon, baking soda, nuts, etc.

Parmesan Tomato Muffins

1 3/4 cups	all-purpose flour	425 mL
1/3 cup	grated Parmesan cheese	75 mL
2 tbsp	granulated sugar	25 mL
2 tsp	baking powder	10 mL
1/4 tsp	baking soda	1 mL
1/8 tsp	garlic powder	.5 mL
1/2 tsp	crushed dried rosemary	2 mL
Dash	black pepper	Dash
1	egg, lightly beaten	1
1/2 cup	milk	125 mL
1/2 cup	tomato sauce	125 mL
1/3 cup	olive oil *or* vegetable oil	75 mL
	Grated Parmesan cheese	

Preheat oven to 350° F (180° C)
Muffin tin, lightly greased

1. In a large bowl, combine flour, cheese, sugar, baking powder, baking soda, garlic powder, rosemary and pepper. Make a well in the center.

2. In another bowl, mix together egg, milk, tomato sauce and oil. Add to dry ingredients, stirring just until moistened and blended. Do not overmix.

3. Spoon batter into prepared muffin tin, filling cups to the top. Bake in preheated oven for 20 to 25 minutes or until lightly browned.

Pepper, Corn and Zucchini Muffins

3/4 cup	all-purpose flour	175 mL
1/3 cup	yellow cornmeal	75 mL
1 tbsp	firmly packed light brown sugar	15 mL
2 tsp	baking powder	10 mL
1/2 tsp	salt	2 mL
1/2 cup	skim milk	125 mL
1	egg	1
1/3 cup	margarine, melted	75 mL
1 1/2 cups	shredded zucchini	375 mL
1/2 cup	chopped roasted red peppers	125 mL

Preheat oven to 400° F (200° C)
Muffin tin, paper-lined

1. In a large bowl, combine flour, cornmeal, sugar, baking powder and salt. Make a well in the center.

2. In another bowl, whisk together milk, egg and melted margarine. Add to dry ingredients, stirring just until moistened and blended. Do not overmix. Stir in zucchini and peppers.

3. Spoon batter into prepared muffin tin. Bake in preheated oven for 20 to 25 minutes.

Cocoa Nut Zucchini Muffins

3/4 cup	butter *or* margarine	175 mL
2 cups	granulated sugar	500 mL
2 tsp	vanilla	10 mL
3	eggs	3
1 1/2 cups	all-purpose flour	375 mL
1 cup	whole-wheat flour	250 mL
1/2 cup	cocoa	125 mL
2 1/2 tsp	baking powder	12 mL
1 1/2 tsp	baking soda	7 mL
1 tsp	cinnamon	5 mL
2 cups	grated zucchini	500 mL
1/2 cup	milk	125 mL
1 cup	chopped nuts	250 mL

Preheat oven to 375° F (190° C)
Muffin tin, greased

1. In a large bowl, cream together butter, sugar and vanilla. Add eggs one at a time, beating well after each addition.

2. In another bowl, combine all-purpose flour, whole-wheat flour, cocoa, baking powder, baking soda and cinnamon. Add to the creamed mixture alternately with zucchini and milk, mixing well. Do not overmix. Fold in nuts.

3. Spoon batter into prepared muffin tin, filling cups to the top. Bake in preheated oven for 25 minutes.

HINT: To clean oven spills, sprinkle with automatic dishwashing powder, cover with wet paper towels and let stand for a few hours. Wipe with a damp sponge.

Graham Muffin Gems

1 cup	all-purpose flour	250 mL
3/4 tsp	salt	4 mL
4 tsp	baking powder	20 mL
4 tbsp	packed brown sugar	50 mL
1 cup	graham flour	250 mL
1 cup	milk	250 mL
1	egg, slightly beaten	1
4 tbsp	butter or margarine, melted	50 mL

Preheat oven to 425° F (220° C)
Muffin tin, greased or paper-lined

1. In a large bowl, mix together all-purpose flour, salt and baking powder. Add brown sugar and graham flour. Add milk, egg and melted butter, stirring just until blended.

2. Spoon batter into prepared muffin tin, filling cups to the top. Bake in preheated oven for about 20 minutes.

VARIATION

 Pecan Muffins: Add 1/2 cup (125 mL) chopped pecan nuts to the dry ingredients. Put a half pecan on each muffin top before baking.

Spreads and Toppings

There are numerous ways to add flavor, variety and a little intrigue to your muffins. Warm sliced muffins are delicious topped with any of the following recipes. Whether added before or after baking, toppings make an extra special treat.

Toppings you can sprinkle on top of muffins *before* baking:

- Sesame or poppy seeds
- Grated Cheddar cheese
- Sugar mixed with lemon or orange zest

Toppings you can sprinkle on top of muffins *after* baking:

- Marmalade, jelly or jam
- Dip tops in melted butter and then in sugar or cinnamon
- Icing sugar
- Chocolate sauce (In a bowl blend together 1 can Eagle Brand milk, 2 squares semi-sweet chocolate, 2 tbsp (25 mL) butter and 1 tsp (5 mL) butter. Heat over low heat.)

Some of the following recipes may seem to yield a large amount, but you will want to have plenty on hand to serve with different flavors of muffins.

Some recipes call for pouring mixture into hot, sterilized jars (using a boiling water bath). Here's the why and how. This process is recommended for acidic foods such as fruits, tomatoes and pickles. It helps to maintain color and flavor and to prevent spoilage. Choose a pan deep enough to allow 1 to 2 inches (2.5 to 5 cm) of water above tops of jars, plus a little extra space for boiling. A roasting pan may be good for this. (Do not use a pressure cooker.) The pan should have a tight-fitting cover and a wire rack to keep jars from touching each other or the sides of the pan. Before preparing your recipe, put pan of water over heat. The water should be boiling when the jars are put in. After jars are filled and lids tightened, immerse them in the hot water, cover pan tightly and bring water quickly back to boiling. Start counting processing time when water again comes to a boil after adding jars. Follow your recipe directions for timing. Set jars upright, 2 to 3 inches (5 to 7.5 cm) apart, on several thicknesses of towels or on a wire rack to cool.

Apple and Plum Butter

4 1/2 lbs	apples	2.25 kg
3 lbs	plums	1.5 kg
2 cups	water	500 mL
6 cups	granulated sugar	1.5 L
1 tsp	cinnamon	5 mL

Makes 6 jars

1. Wash and chop apples and plums. In a saucepan over medium heat, combine chopped apples and plums (including peels and cores) with water and cook until fruit is tender.

2. In a food processor, purée fruit mixture and then push through a sieve. Return to heat. Add sugar and cinnamon. Cook until thick and clear, stirring occasionally to prevent sticking. Fill sterilized jars and seal.

Cinnamon Butter

3 tbsp	softened butter	45 mL
1/2 cup	confectioner's sugar	125 mL
1/4 tsp	cinnamon	1 mL

Makes 1/2 cup (125 mL) butter

1. In a bowl cream together butter, sugar and cinnamon. Chill.

Honey Peach Butter

Great with hot muffins right out of the oven.

1/2 cup	softened butter	125 mL
6 tbsp	peach preserves	90 mL
2 tsp	honey	10 mL

1. In a bowl, beat butter until fluffy. Mix in peach preserves and honey.

HINT: Keep honey or molasses from sticking to the measuring cup by greasing cup first. If recipe calls for vegetable oil, measure that first.

Delicious on peanut butter muffins as well as many others.

Special Fruit Butter

1 cup	puréed baby fruit (any flavor)	250 mL
1 cup	softened butter	250 mL
2 tbsp	icing sugar	25 mL

1. In a bowl, beat together puréed fruit and butter. Beat in sugar. Chill and serve.

Sweet Orange Butter

1/4 cup	softened butter	50 mL
1/2 cup	icing sugar	125 mL
	Juice of half an orange	
	Grated zest of half an orange	

1. In a bowl mix together butter and icing sugar. Add juice and zest. Mix well and serve.

HINT: For lump-free icing sugar (confectioner's sugar), try sifting it through a tea strainer.

Apricot Raspberry Jam

2 lbs	fresh ripe apricots, peeled, pitted and washed	1 kg
2 cups	fresh raspberries, washed	500 mL
2 lbs 4 oz	granulated sugar	1.25 kg
1/4 cup	water	50 mL
1 tbsp	lemon juice	15 mL

1. In a saucepan over medium heat, combine apricots, raspberries, sugar and water. Cook, stirring occasionally, until mixture is thick. (Test by putting a little on a cold plate. If syrup stiffens as soon as it is cool, the jam is done.)

2. Add lemon juice and mix together. Pour jam into hot, sterilized jars and seal with parafin wax.

NOTE: You can make your own jam with any fruit you like in small or large amounts.

Use 1 lb (500 g) (weighed after fruit is prepared) to 1 1/2 cups (375 mL) sugar.

For apple plus another fruit, use 12 oz (375 g) apples and 4 oz (125 g) of another fruit such as peaches, apricots and raspberries.

Light Strawberry Jam

8 cups	halved strawberries	2 L
1 cup	granulated sugar	250 mL
1/2 cup	corn syrup	125 mL
2 tbsp	lemon juice	25 mL

1. In a bowl crush 4 cups (1 L) strawberries with a potato masher.

2. In a saucepan over medium heat, combine crushed strawberries, remaining strawberries and 1/2 cup (125 mL) water; bring to a boil. Reduce heat and simmer, covered, for 10 minutes. Stir in sugar, corn syrup and lemon juice. Increase heat and bring to a boil, stirring constantly. Allow to boil hard, uncovered, for 15 to 20 minutes or until softly set.

3. Remove from heat. Skim off any foam that has risen to the surface. Pour into hot, sterilized jars, leaving 1/2 inch (1 cm) headspace. Seal and process in boiling water bath for 10 minutes.

4. Cool on racks. Store in a cool, dark place. Once jam jars are open, keep in refrigerator for up to 4 weeks.

VARIATION

Peach Apricot Jam: Substitute 4 cups (1 L) each of chopped, peeled peaches and apricots for the strawberries. Reduce lemon juice to 1 tbsp (15 mL).

HINT: Ripen peaches and pears quickly. Place in a brown paper bag with a ripe apple. Keep in a cool place. Make sure there are a few holes in the bag. The apple gives off a gas which stimulates other fruit to ripen.

Grandma's Raspberry Jam

4 cups	fresh ripe raspberries	1 L
1 tbsp	vinegar	15 mL
4 cups	granulated sugar	1 L

Makes 4 or 5 jars
Preheat oven to 275° F (140° C)

1. Put berries in a sieve and quickly run under cold water. (Not for too long as raspberries absorb water easily.) Remove stems.

2. Take 3 pie plates and divide the sugar equally between them. Heat pie plates with sugar on them in preheated oven for 20 minutes.

3. In a large saucepan over medium heat, combine berries and vinegar. Allow to boil, without stirring, for 5 minutes. Add hot sugar, one plate at a time. (Adding the hot sugar this way does not stop the boiling). Boil over high heat for exactly 2 minutes.

4. Pour jam into hot, sterilized jars. Wax and seal.

HINT: Butter the bottom of the saucepan before starting to make jam to prevent it from sticking while cooking. Use a wooden spoon for stirring. Use a metal spoon to remove scum as it accumulates around edges of pan.

Strawberry Rhubarb Jam

3 cups	fresh strawberries	750 mL
2 cups	thickly sliced rhubarb	500 mL
3 cups	granulated sugar	750 mL
3 tbsp	lemon juice	45 mL

1. In a large bowl, crush strawberries 1 cup (250 mL) at a time with a potato masher. Transfer to a large, heavy saucepan. Add the rhubarb. Heat over medium-high heat for 10 minutes or until rhubarb is softened.

2. Reduce heat to low. Stir in sugar and lemon juice until sugar is dissolved. Increase heat to high and bring to a full rolling boil, stirring often. Boil hard, uncovered, for 8 minutes, stirring often. Remove from heat. Let jam cool for 5 minutes, skimming off foam and stirring often.

3. Spoon into jars, leaving 1/2 inch (1 cm) headspace. Cool slightly for 2 minutes. Seal with parafin wax. Tighten lids, cool and store in a cool, dry, dark place.

HINT: To freeze fresh strawberries for making jam later, hull the amount required and freeze on a tray. Place frozen strawberries in freezer bag, remove air and seal. Instead, you could crush fresh berries with a potato masher and freeze in 4-cup (1 L) amounts.

A combination of rhubarb, pineapple and strawberries makes a delicious jam.

3 cups	shredded fresh pineapple	750 mL
2 cups	diced peeled rhubarb	500 mL
4 cups	strawberries, washed and hulled	1 L
Pinch	salt	Pinch
	Juice of 1 lemon	
4 1/2 cups	granulated sugar	1.125 L

Three-Fruit Jam

Preheat oven to 325° F (160° C)
Three pie plates

1. In a Dutch oven, cook pineapple over medium heat for 10 minutes. Add rhubarb, strawberries, salt and lemon juice. Boil gently for 20 minutes.

2. Meanwhile, spread sugar in bottom of pie plates. Heat in preheated oven until sugar is quite hot. (This is done so as not to stop the boiling when added to the fruit). Add heated sugar to fruit mixture. Boil rapidly, stirring often, for 20 to 25 minutes. Skim off any foam.

3. Pour jam into hot, sterilized jars. Seal with hot wax, cover and store in a cool, dry, dark place.

HINT: When making jam, boil fruit gently until cooked before adding the sugar. If the sugar is added before fruit boils, much more is needed. Overboiling the fruit after adding the sugar will adversely affect the flavor, color and consistency.

Nectarine Marmalade

1	orange	1
1	lemon	1
1 cup	water	250 mL
	Juice of 1 lemon	
2 lbs	ripe nectarines or peaches	1 kg
5 cups	granulated sugar	1.25 L
Half	bottle liquid pectin	Half

1. In a blender or food processor, grind orange and lemon with water. Transfer mixture to a saucepan and add juice. Bring to a boil over medium heat. Allow to boil, covered, for 20 minutes.

2. Into a pot of boiling water, drop nectarines. Allow to boil for 20 seconds, then remove from heat. Transfer to a bowl of cold water for half an hour or until cool. Remove nectarines, peel and chop. Add to citrus mixture and boil hard for 2 minutes. Add pectin and boil until a jelly thermometer reaches 221° F (112° C).

3. Remove from heat. Stir and skim off foam for about 10 minutes. Pour into hot, sterilized jars and seal.

Orange (Citrus) Marmalade

8	oranges, washed	8
2	lemons, washed	2
	Water	
2 cups	granulated sugar	500 mL

1. Cut the unpeeled oranges and lemons into quarters lengthwise and then slice very thinly crosswise. Measure the sliced fruit, transfer to a bowl and add twice as much water as fruit and juice. Let stand overnight.

2. The next day, transfer mixture to a pot and bring to a boil. Cook for 1 hour, then set aside for 24 hours.

3. After 24 hours, stir well and measure out 2 cups (500 mL) juice and fruit. Put into a Dutch oven pot. Add sugar. Bring to a full rolling boil and boil for 9 minutes.

4. Pour into hot, sterilized jars and cool. When cold, cover with melted parafin wax. Seal with tight lids. Repeat procedure with any remaining fruit.

VARIATION

Amber Marmalade: Substitute 1 grapefruit, 1 orange and 1 lemon in place of the fruit listed. Use the same amount of sugar and water.

Creamy Berry Spread

1 cup	strawberries *or* raspberries	250 mL
8 oz	light cream cheese, at room temperature	250 g

1. In a bowl mash strawberries.

2. In another bowl, beat softened cream cheese until fluffy. Stir in mashed berries. Spread on sliced muffins or toast.

Lemon Swirl Spread

1	pkg (3 oz [85 g]) softened cream cheese	1
1/2 cup	softened butter	125 mL
4 cups	confectioner's sugar	1 L
1 tsp	vanilla	5 mL
2 to 3 tsp	grated lemon zest	10 to 15 mL
3 tbsp	lemon juice	45 mL

1. In a bowl, beat together cream cheese, butter, sugar, vanilla, zest and juice until fluffy and spreadable. If necessary, add more lemon juice, 1 tsp (5 mL) at a time. Store in refrigerator up to one week.

NOTE: This makes a large amount, so halve the recipe if you're not planning on using much.

HINT: For a quick topping or spread for muffins, place a soft caramel candy in the bottom of each muffin tin or ramekin. Pour batter over top. Bake as usual and then invert. You'll have a delicious caramel sauce!

Plum Cheese Spread

8 oz	cream cheese	250 g
1/2 cup	shredded mild Cheddar cheese	125 mL
2 tbsp	mayonnaise *or* plain yogurt	25 mL
2 tbsp	plum sauce	25 mL

1. In a blender or food processor, cream together cream cheese and Cheddar cheese until smooth. Add mayonnaise and plum sauce and purée until creamy and thick, but not hard.

Special Holiday Spread

1 cup	raisins	250 mL
1/3 cup	rum	75 mL
1	pkg (8 oz [250 g]) softened cream cheese	1
2 cups	grated sharp Cheddar cheese	500 mL
1/4 tsp	cinnamon	1 mL
1/4 tsp	ground ginger	1 mL

1. In a saucepan over low heat, combine raisins and rum. Heat slowly just until hot. Cool for 15 to 20 minutes.

2. In a large bowl, cream together cream cheese, Cheddar cheese, cinnamon and ginger. Drain raisins, reserving rum. Pour rum into cheese mixture and mix until well blended and smooth. Fold in raisins.

3. Put mixture into jar or container. Store, covered, in refrigerator up to 3 weeks.

HINT: For a quick and easy, sweet spread that is terrific on muffins (or toast), combine equal amounts of softened butter or margarine and honey. Add a little vanilla. Start with a smaller amount, like 1/4 tsp (1 mL) and increase, if desired.

Strawberry Cream Cheese Spread

4 oz	low-fat cream cheese	125 g
2 tbsp	strawberry jam	25 mL

1. In a small bowl, mash cream cheese until softened. Stir in jam and mix well.

NOTE: One tbsp (15 mL) low-fat cream cheese has only 50 calories.

VARIATIONS

 Orange: Replace jam with 1 tbsp (15 mL) thawed frozen orange juice concentrate, and 1 tbsp (15 mL) honey.

 Cinnamon Date: Replace jam with 2 tbsp (25 mL) finely chopped dates and 1/4 tsp (1 mL) cinnamon.

 Cinnamon Raisin: Replace jam with 2 tbsp (25 mL) chopped raisins and 1/4 tsp (1 mL) cinnamon.

Nut Crunch Topping

1/4 cup	firmly packed brown sugar	50 mL
1/4 cup	chopped walnuts	50 mL
1 tbsp	all-purpose flour	15 mL
1 tbsp	softened margarine	15 mL
1 tsp	cinnamon	5 mL

1. In a bowl combine brown sugar, walnuts, flour, margarine and cinnamon. Sprinkle over batter. Bake as directed in muffin recipe.

NOTE: This recipe can also be used as a filling for muffins.

Sugar-Cinnamon Mix

1/3 cup	granulated sugar	75 mL
1 1/2 tsp	cinnamon	7 mL
1 tbsp	margarine, melted	15 mL

1. In a bowl combine sugar, cinnamon and margarine. Sprinkle over batter. Bake as directed in muffin recipe.

HINT: Keep muffins hot longer by lining your basket (under the cloth or napkin) with a sheet of foil.

Chocolate, Sour Cream and Coconut Topping

1 cup	semi-sweet chocolate pieces	250 mL
1 cup	sour cream	250 mL
1/4 cup	toasted coconut	50 mL
1 tsp	vanilla	5 mL

1. In top of a double boiler over hot water, melt chocolate. Add sour cream, stirring until well blended. Add coconut and vanilla and mix well.

HINT: Buy or make molded chocolate cups. Fill them with ice-cream, drizzle with a sauce or liqueur that compliments the ice cream flavor.

Crunchy Broiled Topping

1/4 cup	softened butter	50 mL
2/3 cup	firmly packed brown sugar	150 mL
1/2 cup	finely chopped nuts	125 mL
1/2 cup	Whole Wheat Flakes cereal	125 mL
3 tbsp	milk	45 mL

1. In a bowl cream together butter and brown sugar. Add nuts and cereal, mixing well. Stir in milk, mixing until well blended.

2. Spread evenly over muffins, hot from the oven. Put under broiler for 3 minutes or until topping is bubbling and slightly browned.

Lemon Glaze Topping

1 cup	icing sugar	250 mL
2 to 3 tsp	grated lemon zest	10 to 15 mL
4 to 5 tsp	lemon juice	20 to 25 mL

1. In a bowl combine icing sugar and lemon zest. Add lemon juice gradually, mixing well until desired consistency is reached.

Peach Walnut Topping

1 cup	peach preserves	250 mL
1 tbsp	butter *or* margarine	15 mL
	Juice of 1 orange	
1/4 cup	chopped walnuts	50 mL

1. In a small saucepan over low heat, combine peach preserves, butter and orange juice. Cook, stirring, until heated and blended. Stir in walnuts. Serve warm.

Streusel Topping

1/3 cup	softened butter or margarine	75 mL
1/3 cup	granulated sugar	75 mL
1/2 cup	all-purpose flour	125 mL
1 cup	ground dry cake or bread crumbs	250 mL
1 tsp	cinnamon	5 mL

1. In a bowl cream butter while gradually adding sugar. Mix well. Add flour, crumbs and cinnamon, stirring until well mixed and crumbly.

2. Spoon topping over batter. Bake as directed in muffin recipe.

HINT: If you want a quick and delicious icing for carrot muffins boil a small potato and mash it. Add icing sugar and vanilla.

Toffee Coffee Topping

1 cup	packed brown sugar	250 mL
2 tbsp	cornstarch	25 mL
Pinch	salt	Pinch
1 3/4 cups	hot strong coffee	425 mL
2 tbsp	butter *or* margarine	25 mL
2 tsp	vanilla	10 mL

1. In a heavy saucepan over low heat, combine brown sugar, cornstarch and salt. Add coffee and cook, stirring, until thickened. Remove from heat. Add butter and vanilla, stirring until well blended. Drizzle warm over muffins.

Whipped Cream Topping

1 cup	whipping (35%) cream	250 mL
2 to 4 tbsp	confectioner's sugar	25 to 60 mL

1. In a bowl, beat together cream and sugar until stiff.

VARIATIONS

Grand Marnier: To unbeaten cream add 1 to 2 tbsp (15 to 25 mL) icing sugar and 2 tbsp (25 mL) orange liqueur. Beat until stiff.

Mocha: To unbeaten cream add 1/4 cup (50 mL) icing sugar, 3 tbsp (45 mL) unsweetened cocoa powder, 1 tsp (5 mL) instant coffee granules and 1/2 tsp (2 mL) vanilla. Beat until stiff.

Peppermint: To unbeaten cream add 2 tbsp (25 mL) icing sugar, a drop of green food coloring and 1/4 tsp (1 mL) peppermint extract. Beat until stiff.

Strawberry: To unbeaten cream add a drop of red food coloring and 2 tbsp (25 mL) strawberry jam. Beat until stiff.

HINT: To test doneness of jam or jelly, place a small plate in the freezer section of your refrigerator for an hour before you start cooking. Place a small spoonful of the boiling jam or jelly on the cold plate. Let it cool for a few seconds. Hold plate up vertically. If jam stays on the plate, it is cooked.

HINT: Store your favorite muffin recipes neatly by slipping them between the clear plastic pages of a photo album. They are protected from spills and can be removed easily.

Index